ANOTHER WORLD

Poetry & Art by Young People

FROM *THE POETRY STUDIO*

Ann Gengarelly
&
Tony Gengarelly

FOREWORD BY CHARD deNIORD
Poet Laureate of Vermont, 2015-2019

LUMINARE PRESS

WWW.LUMINAREPRESS.COM

ANOTHER WORLD
Poetry and Art by Young People from The Poetry Studio

Printed in the United States of America

Preface by Ann Gengarelly, copyright 2021

Foreword by Chard deNiord, copyright 2021

"Birthing Poetry" by Ann Gengarelly, copyright 2021

"Word and Image" by Tony Gengarelly, copyright 2021

Cover Design and Interior Layout by Claire Flint Last

Editing: Bobolink Communications (bobolinkvermont.com)

Cover Photograph: Aashna Kinkhabwala
writing in the gardens at *The Poetry Studio*

Production Support: The Jessica Park Project at
Massachusetts College of Liberal Arts (www.mcla.edu/JessicaPark)

Photographs and Images courtesy of *The Poetry Studio* (thepoetrystudiovt.com)

The Poetry Studio logo design courtesy of Good Bear Productions
(goodbearproductions.com) and the artwork of Frida Rosner

LUMINARE PRESS
442 Charnelton St. Eugene, OR 97401
www.luminarepress.com

LCCN: 2021913861
ISBN: 978-1-64388-778-4

Dedication

Love and appreciation beyond measure to the young people who have been the impetus and inspiration for this book. Profound gratitude not only for their extraordinary poetry and art, but also for the in-between spaces where earnest and lively conversations invited us to explore the many dimensions of the human condition.

Ultimately words can never do justice to the process that takes place in the creation of making a poem or drawing. There is a mystery here we can never fathom, let alone put into words. What we do know is our deep admiration for the students' poems and art that sing from these pages.

The privilege of sitting with a student who has one foot on Earth, the other often in the magical world of spirit* connects us to an intuitive knowing, a reminder to rehabilitate the idea of our larger nature.

In so many ways, these young people have become our teachers: When the uncertainty of life assails us, how fortunate we are for these wise ones who invent maps to navigate our world, both beautiful and bewildering.

* Inspired by: Tobin Hart, *The Secret Spiritual World of Children* (Inner Ocean 2003)

Table of Contents

Poetry and Art by Young People

CHAPTER ONE
Journeys & Transformations

CHAPTER TWO
Nature as Teacher & Nature as Metaphor

CHAPTER THREE
Nature Characters & Conversations with Nature

CHAPTER FOUR
Stretching Borders

CHAPTER FIVE
Animal Magic & Magical Creatures

CHAPTER SIX
Mythical Worlds & Mythic Beings

CHAPTER SEVEN
Who Am I? Who Are We?

Reflections

Another World

This must be another world
far from the blood and the violence
sheltered from pain and death.
Poppy, scarlet chalice
can have nothing to do with our blood-stained newsprint.
These gentle flowers, white-frilled trumpets
have no relation to our drums of war.
The beauty of a purple iris,
tall and stately,
stands unconnected to hate
unshadowed by murder or disease.
The unmarked purity
of a white peony, petals tightly knotted,
shielding leaves beginning
to curl slowly away
is not related to anger or guns,
and the daylilies,
tender golden trumpets,
do not voice
the harsh call of war.

HANNAH CHRISTENSEN
Written at *The Poetry Studio* at age 10

PREFACE

By Ann Gengarelly

The seat of the soul is where the inner world
And the outer world meet…
—NOVALIS
(translated by Robert Bly, *News of the Universe*,
Sierra Club Books 1980)

In 1995 *The Poetry Studio* opened its doors to young people, ranging in age from 5-17, for after-school programs and summer workshops. Located on beautiful grounds in Marlboro, Vermont, *The Poetry Studio* provides an intimate lens through which to see the natural world and inspire a deep communion with nature. Offering their devoted attention to the scent of pine needles after a long night of rain, to the patient unfolding of hibiscus blossoms, students are surrounded by rich imagery that finds expression in both poetry and art. The studio atmosphere invites a marriage between inner and outer landscapes, where imagination and discovery are often imbued with magic. A stone walkway becomes a metaphor for the poet's sense of time. A *Twilight Princess* "is called once more / to paint the sky with crimson, lay down the dawn to sleep."*

Keeping the company of young people, we are convinced that everyone has a need to tell their stories; everyone needs to express themselves. Poetry and art become gateways that lead to journeys where students explore territory that denies "ordinary speech." To offer a shape to the loss of innocence, the injustices of the world, relationships with family and friends, the many facets of love and grief can help to compose more *awake* and conscious beings and hopefully a kinder world.

What an honor it is to accompany these young poets and artists on their travels. Their capacity for wonder and wisdom, for compassion and deep questioning, and for seeing beneath the surface of the physical world lifts us beyond the mundane. Along with them, we experience the extraordinary ability to enter invisible realms, often crossing over bridges to mystery.

* from *The Twilight Princess* by Linaea DiMarino, written at age 13

The Poetry Studio Entrance

The illustrations and decorative book pages have a visual relationship with the words and expand the environment in which the poet is working. Often amplifying the language, these compelling images are works of art in their own right that move us to another level of appreciation.

Over the years we have been graced by the students' inspired work. So many poems and drawings/paintings cover the walls of *The Poetry Studio*; on various bookshelves colorful scrapbooks hold seasons of poetry and art. Our gratitude embraces all the students who have opened our hearts, whose arresting images have slipped into the bloodstream of many, indelible words and images deeply rooted in our collective memories.

The selection process for this book was difficult, because many exceptional poems and beautifully rendered drawings could not be included. Their absence does not suggest that a particular piece of writing or art is not "good enough." Ultimately, we focused on a range of voices and imagery to be shared with the larger community: poems that dare to take remarkable leaps; art of surprising imagination and original-ity; poems and visual depictions that speak to the human condition; poems and art

The Poetry Studio: Erin LeBlanc Writing by the Frog Pond

where we feel the poet/artist's kinship with a tree, a plant—this connection inviting the kind of harmony, balance about which indigenous people speak.

This book reaches out to other young people who may well discover parts of themselves in these pages. Very quickly these poems and works of art invite an *I-Thou* connection; a word, a phrase, an image that immediately resonates with the reader. Being a witness for many years to the beauty, the wisdom, the grief that often dwells in the young people's poetry and art, we hope teachers, parents, aunts, grandparents, counselors, librarians will see a dimension of young people not always recognized or valued. This recognition is especially critical in our culture where the voices of our youth can be easily drowned by the cacophony of what seems important. In our world where vulnerability can be perceived as weakness, at *The Poetry Studio* we bow to the students who travel inward and courageously offer messages of the heart. May this book summon us from the myriad distractions of our lives to encounters of healing and illumination.

FOREWORD

By Chard deNiord,
Vermont Poet Laureate (2015-2019)

The late Brazilian poet Carlos Drummond de Andrade wrote in his famous poem "Friendly Song": "I am working on a song / that will awaken men / and make children sleep." But what happens to adults, one might ask as a logical afterthought to Andrade's *ars poetica,* when a child "works" on his or her "song"? The poems in *Another World* provide wondrous answers to this question by testifying repeatedly in evocative, stunning ways to William Wordsworth's claim that "the child is the father of the man." And mother, too, one needs to add as an overdue update to this maxim.

The poems in this anthology by young poets between the ages of five and seventeen sound the always timely "alarm" that Walt Whitman celebrates in the visionary child who ventures "forth every day" and becomes "the first object" he or she looks upon with the consequence of that object becoming "a part of him [or her] for the day or a certain part of the day, / Or for many years or stretching cycles of years." The inspired equations these young poets make with others in their communion with nature and their fellow human beings are memorable in ways that are less precocious than simply wise in their piercing insights, verbal economy, figurative leaps, and lack of what John Keats called "irritable reaching." Here are just a few examples:

Before the earth was born,
before I became myself
I was the Bird of Beauty and Health.
I had a fawn's head,
a hummingbird's body,
a peacock's tail.

From "How I Became Myself"
by Lila Blau
Written at age 8

Little pine...
teach me to love the stone
that blocks my path;
teach me to stand
even when cast into darkness;
teach me to protect the spider
unconditionally
and ask for nothing in return.

From "Little Pine" by Ellie Friends
Written at age 13

My skin is as smooth
as the inside of a shell.
My eyes are the color
of peppercorns
and as bright as the stars.

Inside I have silence,
a quiet like a fallen petal.

When I'm quiet
I sit in a rocking chair
dreaming about summer
on a windy, winter day.

My inside is warm
with love and kindness.

Ann says I listen as carefully
as a deer listening
for the rustle of leaves.

From "Myself"
by Louisa Eichelberger
Written at age 5

In addition to these examples of inspired compassion and the transpersonal self, the young poets in *Another World* exhibit an impressive array of self-effacing, hopeful verses that remind the reader of Socrates's famous adage: "the unexamined life is not worth living." In deft, transformative language, these young poets find magical ways to conjure explosive lines of verbal "alarms" that wake their elders to truths they didn't know they knew, or had simply forgotten in their adult sleep, as in these poems:

The wise man was wrong.
The crack in my heart only grew.
The place in between is a city of sadness.

From "A Mistake of the Wise Man" by Frida Rosner
Written at age 12

Last November, I saw my doubt in a wolf's body.
He turned his head sharply,
eyes an icy blue
and thick, gray fur, soft like wings.
Then he ducked under the trees,
tail nodding in the wind.
But I still see him dawdling
in the throat of my mind.

From "Never Without You" by Claire Holmes
Written at age 12

They say my dark side
overcame me, that my thoughts
for the world are bitter and cold.
They say I'm the darkest at night,
but at night my love shines purest.
At night I run through sacred fields of ancestors,
befriend the stars before they burst
at dawn, we sing to each other songs
of ancient memories.
At twilight I sit
on the big dipper, my long
raven hair is blown
by the wind to create
the shadow that will cause
the night to begin.

"Daughter of the Milky Way"
by Maise Sperling
Written at age 12

One comes away from reading the poems in *Another World* with a renewed sense of hope and amazement in the innate wisdom of children's grasp of literal and figurative language in addressing their relation to themselves, to others, to beauty, and to the vast array of specific, inscrutable mysteries surrounding them in the disguise of the ordinary. Loew Lumbra Armstrong, age 8, speaks for his fellow poets and artists about his creative experience at *The Poetry Studio,* and in so doing captures the irrepressible, necessary activity all people, no matter how young or old, need to preserve their essential humanity:

There is a boy
who loves poetry.
The boy only receives good poems
if he listens to his heart.
The boy feels mindful and peaceful
as an oak tree standing still
in the middle of a long grassy meadow.
When the boy opens
the door to The Poetry Studio
he knows many poems
will spread throughout his whole body,
every Wednesday
and every fall.
The boy feels joyful.

"There is a boy…"
 by Loew Lumbra Armstrong
Written at age 8

*Songs are thoughts, sung out with the breath when people are moved
by great forces and ordinary speech no longer suffices.*

—Orpingalik, Inuit poet

*Isn't man wonderful? He longed so much to speak his heart that he taught
himself language, so that what was inside him could be spoken to the world.*

—Sophocles,
Antigone

*What needs to be counted on to have a voice?
Courage. Anger. Love. Something to say; someone to speak to;
someone to listen... In a voiced community we all flourish.*

—Terry Tempest Williams,
When Women Were Birds

*Where do we allow space for young people to access and articulate their sense
of power and purpose, their vulnerability and their courage?*

—Gillian Huebner, from Krista Tippet,
On Being: Living the Question, July 2018

Birthing Poetry

By Ann Gengarelly

Reading the poems in *Another World,* we have the rare privilege to witness voices that amaze, that embody wisdom, that remind us of the beauty in the world. We also discover a depth of grief; grief from feeling isolated; grief about the absence of attention to the environment; grief about the loss of innocence which ultimately becomes a lament, an urgent plea for adults to listen:

> *I have seen the bleak routine patterns*
> *of human nature.*
> *Time around us was like*
> *a carefully picked judgment.*
> *As adults forgot they were adults,*
> *kids stopped hoping.*
> *They just waited and watched,*
> *their tongues hanging out*
> *like dogs looking for love.*
>
> *And we watched,*
> *hoping we were more innocent*
> *than we felt.*

Ezra Marder
Written at age 14

The unique language of poetry allows emotions and insights to find a voice often denied by "ordinary speech." As one student proclaimed: "I can write what I cannot speak." That sentiment is echoed by many, young and old. I remember a fifth-grade girl who wrote an ode to her friend; in our final sharing circle, the poet read her piece out loud. Twenty-five years later I can still hear what her friend said: "I never knew you felt that way." And the poet replied: "I couldn't have told you any other way."

The Mexican poet Octavio Paz tells us that "without poetry we would forget ourselves." This extraordinary collection, *Another World*, reveals how poetry offers authentic voices that dig deep in the soil of remembering who we are. We are summoned to recall the human condition and the inner song that finds a home in poetry. Page after page, these poems reveal connections between the poet's inner landscape and the world outside:

> *Emotions are like the rings of a tree,*
> *One inside the other,*
> *Working together to create one's soul.*

> Ella Bathory-Peeler
> from *The Emotion Tree*
> Written at age 14

Over the years, many have been astonished by the wisdom and insight expressed in these young poets' voices and have wondered how their poems were created. Although the creative process ultimately remains a mystery, hopefully part of the mystery will unfold as we travel through the poets' rich terrain in the making of their poems.

When a graduate student decides to do an internship at *The Poetry Studio*, I find myself saying: "I don't have any formula for how I teach." Rather the question of how to create environments where young people's voices can flourish is visited again and again. In this respect my work is very intentional and specific rituals punctuate our time together.

Imagine students walking into *The Poetry Studio*, gathering in a circle, greeting one another. It doesn't take long for a warm and welcoming tone to be felt by all. In many ways we cross over a threshold and enter a ritual space where everyone offers their best selves to one another. Sometimes we sit in a group of five; sometimes seventeen. Often during our first class I ask the students to consider the word *reverence* and what that word means to them; for some an easier translation is the word respect. A rich dialogue takes place and a list is created: reverence for who we are, for our authentic voices and those of our peers; reverence for the natural environment, for *The Poetry Studio* and the gardens that surround it. Establishing the critical nature of reverence helps to create a safe environment where students of all ages dare to write about whatever is begging for a voice.

It is during this first circle that I offer a theme that might capture the students' imaginations. Portraits, for instance, opens the door to a wide range of possibilities: self-portraits; invented characters; a portrait of a friend, a family member. I also introduce a variety of poems related to the theme. Joseph Bruchach's poem *Birdfoot's Grampa* is a perfect example of how the poet uses vivid imagery to portray the "inside" of a character. The specific detail of the old man "stopping his car two dozen times / to save the toads"—says everything about the man's kindness and compassion. When I read poems such as this one, students can barely restrain their enthusiasm, exclaiming: "I really like the last line: 'They have places to go too.'" When I ask, "How do you know that he is an old man?" many—especially younger students call out: "leathery hands," "a mist around his white hair."

This offering of a theme is a way to stir up the creative juices and to provide an anchor in a sea of possibilities for writing. It is never a frame into which students must fit their voices. Always there is the opportunity for students to stray from the theme; "to turn inward"[1] and to pay attention to whatever is critical for releasing their inner thoughts and feelings. In a Toltec poem, there is a line, "The true artist / maintains dialogue with his heart." These words from the poem *The Words Out of My Mouth* by 15-year-old Frida Rosner remind us of what loss feels like:

> *I realized I was a cut flower*
> *when his anger-filled eyes came to rest upon me*
> *and I wilted a little.*

An 8-year-old boy walks into the studio announcing, "I know what I want to write about! 'Poetry is like Love Armies'" (Samuel Garbarino, p. 30). That knowing is the clay that often shapes a good poem. In this instance, as in many others, the teacher becomes a midwife, helping to bring forth what already dwells within. How a first line or a salient image arrives from "somewhere else" often remains unknown. What I do believe is that the poet and teacher dwell in a moment, rare and intimate, where we recognize something powerful is transpiring at the intersection of our lives.

The experience of a young student receiving a poem is not so different from that of many writers who feel certain poems have mysteriously arrived, that a poem was given to them by some unnamable force. There is a well-known story about Vermont poet Ruth Stone who described how she would be out walking in the fields and could sense a poem coming. If she ran to her house and wrote the words down, the poem was hers. At the same time, if she didn't catch the poem, it would move on to another poet. I don't know about any poem landing in another student's heart, but I certainly have witnessed the sensation and exhilaration when a young poet bursts into *The Poetry Studio,* as Samuel did with his poem.

After the initial circle, students disperse and discover a spot to which they are drawn. Some settle in at the art table where watercolor pencils, paints, and collage material are available. Younger students especially use visual imagery to begin their journey into a poem. Sometimes if the mood doesn't invite a poem, a student may spend the entire hour and more on a piece of art. Others find different places to begin their writing: a colorful pillow on the floor or the couch to sit on; in good weather, a bench by the frog pond. They may lie on a ledge where they can listen for the song of the wind or the voice of a rock.

Students of all ages respond eagerly to the theme *Another Way to Listen,* based on the story by Byrd Baylor. The quiet mood young people sustain as they sit in a patch of grass listening to one blade—or putting their ears to a clump of flowers "chattering and laughing" inspires the rest of us to pause and listen:

> *Listen to the family of black-eyed Susans*
> *sharing their secrets with the maple.*
>
> *Listen to the apple tree*
> *whispering its wisdom to the stone wall.*

> Hillary Leeds, from *Listen to the Willow's Words*
> Written at age 9

In this fast-paced world, *The Poetry Studio* is an oasis for slow time. Students are encouraged to pause, to daydream—to sense the energy of the necessary empty space for words and images that might give birth to a poem. Having spaciousness—not feeling rushed—allows the students to access that part of themselves so often forgotten in their busy lives.

If you were to visit *The Poetry Studio* in summer, spring, or fall, you would see poets walking around the gardens, sitting on one of the decks or nestled in a chair on our porch; you might also notice a teacher sharing a dialogue with a student, a dialogue that is truly a delicate and nuanced process. Some students benefit from this kind of engagement at the onset of writing; some in the midst of writing. The creative process is different for each individual, so as teachers we are especially mindful of a young person's particular rhythm.

Students might say "I need more time —please come back later." Or a student lets us know—either by words or body language—that they are "stuck." In this case a teacher often initiates a discussion about what interests the student or even suggests, among other things, a "poetry walk;" the nature of this walk being that of total silence so they can be aware of the call of a hawk way above or notice the many newts below after a rainy night. For poetry, in many ways, is the invitation to pay attention to the song of the whippoorwill, the shimmer of a raindrop on the leaf of a hosta; even the thought of war.

If one were to listen to a conversation with a student, one might hear some questions shared with the poet. Sometimes when an image fascinates me but might benefit from more detail, I ask *how* or *why.* In *Lion Cub* (p. 120), a poem about an animal that has "magical ears," I remember out of earnest curiosity asking the poet "How are the ears magical?" or "What can the magic do?"

The poet then added these lines:

> *My ears were so magical*
> *they could hear*
> *the whisper of flowers,*
> *the gentle voice of a single leaf*
> *trembling on the oak.*

Rosalie Smith
Written at age 10

Some years back, I had the good fortune to hear Barry Lopez, the renowned naturalist, talk at The Key West Literary Festival. What lingers are his words about the distinction between a tourist and a traveler; how a traveler assumes "the presence of being a guest in someone else's country." For me "being a guest in someone else's country" suggests a reverence for the people's language, rituals, customs.

Joy Harjo, who belongs to the Muscogee Nation and is the first Native American to be named the U. S. Poet Laureate, writes, "When entering another country do not claim ownership."[2]

So it is with the nature of a dialogue shared with a student. What a great honor it is to sit with a poet, to recognize the energy of their poem, questions arising from being a guest in the poet's landscape. Understanding the ripe moment to share a conversation might inspire students to "be able to find a voice that brings a special fire to their writing."[3]

This exchange surely is different from claiming ownership as a result of a teacher imposing their own sensibilities. Listen, for instance to the student's outrage in the poem *Please Don't Hand Me My Soul* (p. 157). Certainly our antennae must be tuned for the depth of imagination, the richness of language articulated by a young poet; our questions and comments shaped by the necessity of being present for what is or is not being offered by the student.

If you were to accompany Maise Sperling on her journey with writing *The Girl Whose Heart Rose into the Sun* (p. 133), you would witness how those words—that later became her title—bubbled out of her mouth as she sat down for a snack before class began.

As we sat together, you might hear her ponder: "Should I use a comparison to stress the girl's belief in the sun's reign?" During our back and forth where I mainly listened, she triumphantly came up with the lines:

> But there was a girl who believed
> In the sun's reign.
> Her belief like a ship anchored
> To the sea of her soul.

In many ways, Maise developed this poem the way an artist creates a collage. At the onset she scribbled words/phrases onto a piece of paper. From time to time, I recorded her words when her intensity and passion might have refused the transition of heart speech onto paper, frustration possibly becoming a barrier. Ultimately this process found its way into the creation of one of Maise's most original and compelling poems.

Imagine a young child who is just learning to write or for whom writing can become a burden and all creative instincts might get lost in the maze of physically placing letter after letter on the blank page. In such instances it is necessary for me or an assistant teacher to act as a scribe for their poetry words. Assuming this role perhaps is the most challenging path to explore. In a way we must inhabit this space with the utmost care, keeping the doors wide open to the house of a young child's imagination. With no way to anticipate what words might be offered or whether we will be greeted by silence, we embody a kind of innocence as we shed the all-knowing, the keeper of right answers. In these moments we practice what Buddhists call "a beginner's mind."[4] When we are ready for anything, we remove the mantle of expert and embrace boundless possibilities. To hold space for surprise, for *not knowing* is the key that allows for an open-heartedness. Sometimes when a student offers an image that stuns my whole being, I find myself exclaiming, "Did you hear what you just said?" In such moments I have the pleasure of holding up a mirror which reflects an extraordinary metaphorical leap:

> *Two souls*
> *that used to be brothers,*
> *now shadowed ghosts.*

> Alban Neil , from *Heaven*
> Written at age 8

Contemplate sitting with 5-year-old Louisa, feeling the pulse of pride and enthusiasm as she shared her self-portrait collage (p. 179). How long we talked I cannot say. At some point, I might have asked, "Do you want to begin your poem describing your 'inside' or your 'outside' or do you have another way to begin?" After Louisa spoke about her "skin as smooth / as the inside of a shell," she began to talk about the quality of her listening, exploring different ways of capturing that special quiet. In my mind Louisa stands on her toes inviting me to be the trusted keeper of her words, whispering in my ear, "I listen as carefully / as a deer listening / for a rustle of leaves."

Students of all ages understand that poetry is the art of using language that surprises. They also understand that poetry is the art of expressing an emotion, an experience with the fewest words possible. Because many of my classes take place in nature—often among the many gardens—young people understand the parallel between weeding a garden and weeding a poem. Beginning at a very young age, students are introduced to what we call "poetry scissors" as a visual prompt, scissors cut from cardboard that are always nearby. Whether a student decides to cut a "tired" word or too many words, the decision is always theirs.

Sometimes when a student can't decide whether or not to use a particular word or whether to repeat a word we might suggest reading the poem out loud or having us read the poem different ways while they sit quietly. The acclaimed poet, Stanley Kunitz, was a strong advocate of this kind of listening. We might encourage students to go outside and read their poem to a tree; to not just say the words but to *feel* them. Often they return with a smile on their face, knowing which direction their poem needs to follow.

These dialogues in no way suggest the kind of editorial revision that might turn a student away from writing poetry. Rather, they become a portal through which a young poet has the opportunity to clarify an image, to be present for what the poem wants. For this to happen, the teacher cannot be attached to a particular outcome for the poem. Honoring the journey of the creative process; the delight of attending to the yeses and nos of a student, we might just find ourselves entering original and illuminating territory. Our students remind us that the act of "poemmaking" is what matters most. The sacred nature of this kind of time spent with a young poet surely cannot be pinned down by words. At best we can recognize signposts for the road we travel together. We can also trust that at a ripe moment many will want to bring a discerning vision to their writing, whether it's recognizing "dead" language or stretching an image to create a more vivid picture in their readers' minds.

Since kindness and earnest respect at *The Poetry Studio* tie us all together, it feels imperative that we also move beyond our familiar borders and recognize through the writing of poems the plight of others. The distinguished poet Denise Levertov writes: "There can be no self-respect without respect for others—and no recognition of others is possible without the imagination. The imagination of what it is to 'be' those other forms of life that want to live is the only way to recognition: and it is that imaginative recognition that brings compassion to birth."[5]

In the summer of 2018 a student wrote the poem *Chains* (p. 165) where she assumed the persona of a slave. This imaginative recognition deepens not only the poet's capacity for compassion but also stretches all of us who listen as her repetition of the word *chains* creates a beat that drums into our souls.

The chains wrapped around my ankles.
The chains wrapped around my happiness.
The chains wrapped around my wrists.
The chains around my tears.

Tae Weiss
Written at age 12

This leap of the imagination reminds me of a third grader who many years ago proclaimed: "I don't feel sad today, but I am going to try sad on." In *Chains,* the poet dwells in the "Halls of Injustice,"[6] embodying the virtue of walking in another's shoes. This *trying on* certainly deepens our capacity for empathy and ultimately transformation.

Another kind of compassion emerges when young people have the opportunity to engage with the gardens and woods that surround them—to develop an *I-Thou* relationship with a particular tree, plant, or bird that pours into their poetry. Surely indigenous people have understood that trees and plants and all sentient beings have spirit; that kind of connection refusing the separation between human and tree, human and plants. Many naturalists concerned about the state of our environment believe that we must come to love nature before we develop the desire to preserve it. Hear the words of a 7-year-old poet:

> *I am the guardian of tree toads,*
> *as small as a raindrop.*
> *They're so small*
> *you might not notice them.*
> *But I hope my grandchildren*
> *and their grandchildren*
> *will see this gift of nature,*
> *tree toads hopping*
> *and leaping through summer grass.*

Willow Weiss
Written at age 7

Poetry offers a dignity to young people's individual stories. In our last circle, when students share their poems and listen to those of others, they feel empowered as poetry reflects their feelings and thoughts and, in turn they have the opportunity to recognize themselves in the images of other people's writing. In many ways an invisible thread ties writer and listener together, making each feel less alone in the world; creating the possibility for rich community, something for which we all hunger.

It is during this final sharing that we consider how a poem read to the group is a gift. We explore the question: What are different ways we can convey our gratitude to a poet? Someone in the circle suggests that a compliment to the poet about a specific word, phrase, image could be helpful—"I like when you said acorn brown, not just brown;" another listener might address the emotional pulse of the writing. With older students, some big ideas surface; for instance, the ephemeral nature of life (see Erin LeBlanc's poem *When Summer Left*, pp. 44-45). Remembering their time at the studio, students often talk about what is especially powerful: many value this last circle where they feel totally heard. Positive support and generous listening, along with an atmosphere of reverence and respect, create the fertile soil from which the real inner voice can emerge.

The recollection of students becoming thoroughly immersed in their writing and sharing brings to mind Seamus Heaney's poem *Digging*. Here we encounter an indelible image of his grandfather digging for potatoes, going "down and down/for the good turf." As the poem reaches its crescendo, the poet Heaney responds:

> *Between my finger and my thumb*
> *The squat pen rests*
> *I'll dig with it.*[7]

The depth to which young poets dig, not only in their writing but also in conversations that sink "down and down," brings up thoughts and feelings that utterly amaze us.

In our culture where technology has the possibility of connecting people, it can also become a substitute for "real" communication, leaving many to feel isolated. An antidote to feeling alone and separate certainly resides in the act of witnessing, a profound experience that occurs on many levels in our classes. First, the poets have the opportunity to witness their own responses as they sit alone, opening themselves to whatever material and experiences will unlock their special concerns, hopes, and dreams. The poem itself bears witness to what the poet thinks and feels. And the teacher becomes a witness too when a dialogue is shared with a student, creating the palpable feeling of being human together. Even though each student writes from their own special place, their "sit spot," I imagine they sense the communal spirit that deepens in the final circle when the young people share their work and others have the privilege to witness the inner voice of the poet. A third grader reads a poem about the death of her dog. Suddenly a crowd of voices enter: "My cat died a month ago." "My uncle died last year." There is the poetry of the poem; the poetry of shared conversation; conversation that forms a circle of humanity.

As we turn the pages of this book, we witness how the poet's gaze turns inward or outward into the universe; how a poem weaves a tapestry of yarns whose colors draw us deeper into the way these young people are reckoning with what has been given to them: not only the world's difficulties, but also the incandescence of summer's bounty or an act of kindness that "sings us awake."[8] What becomes evident is that the process of writing a poem provides an opportunity to reinvent the self, to reinvent the world.

Another World ultimately is a plea to listen deeply to these young people. Their poems are an invitation to generous ears—they are dedicated to anyone who is receptive to learning what our youth truly feel and think, often capturing what is otherwise ineffable. As we struggle to understand the current world in which we find ourselves, to develop a moral compass and to deepen compassion, we might discover a "wellspring very close to home," in the authentic spirit life of young people.[9] Spending intimate time with these poets, we can lean into hope, believing that a more just world is possible; that being "awake" to the self and to the world can be a transformative, healing experience.

Celebrated poet Mary Oliver tells us that "Poetry is old… sacred… a community ritual…. A poem is for anyone or everybody; it's a giving… a gift."[10] Because "the voices of children [have] come breaking their way / to my heart",[11] I felt compelled to share the gift of their voices with the larger community. And so this book was born.

References

1   Rainer Maria Rilke, *Letters to a Young Poet*, p. 18

2   Joy Harjo, *How We Became Human: New and Selected Poems* (W.W. Norton & Co., 2002), p. 155

3   Ann Gengarelly, "Literary Cavalcade," *Scholastic Magazine, 1985,* p. 4

4   Shunryu Suzuki, *Zen Mind, Beginner's Mind* (Weatherhill 1970), pp. 13-14

5   Denise Levertov, *The Poet in the World* (New Directions Books 1960), p. 53

6   Lisel Mueller, *Alive Together; New and Selected Poems* (Louisiana State University Press 1996) "The Laughter of Women."

7   Seamus Heaney, *Digging.*

8   Gregory Orr, *This Is What Was Bequeathed Us.*

9   Tobin Hart, *The Secret Spiritual World of Children (*Inner Ocean 2003), p. 16

10   Mary Oliver, "Listening to the World," Interview by Krista Tippett. *On Being.* NPR. September 2015, https://onbeing.org/programs/mary-oliver-listening-to-the-world/

11   Snehal Vadher, "Beauty is brief and violent," *Poetry,* July/August 2019

At The Poetry Studio, creative practice often begins within a
beautiful garden landscape, providing visual inspiration for poems and
pictures while creating a safe space for "inner work."

Word and Image

By Tony Gengarelly

*A*nother World features a selection of drawings, paintings, and decorative presentations that complement the creative practice that takes place at *The Poetry Studio*, where art supports the expression of language and language inspires art. The studio's walls are covered with students' poetry and related artwork to serve as models of inspiration. Over the past several years, the students' extraordinary combinations of words and images have been featured by commercial and college galleries and displayed in museums throughout southern Vermont, including Massachusetts College of Liberal Arts (fall 2017–spring 2021) and the Brattleboro Museum & Art Center (Sept. 2016–Feb. 2017).

It is important to note that there is no formal art instruction at *The Poetry Studio*. Rather, we facilitate the creative process by supplying appropriate materials and, when requested by the student, model images and/or stencils to help with their drawings. No comments are made that might inhibit a naturally free expression—one hears only encouraging words of support. What a student needs to say in their art is not restrained by the teacher's idea of what is "good or bad" use of color or line or proportion or visual accuracy. Viktor Lowenfeld's seminal study of the development of young people's art, *Creative and Mental Growth*, concludes that "every child is born creative" and needs to be free to develop that creativity: "Art has been traditionally interpreted as relating to the study of aesthetics, and this concept has in some cases limited the opportunity for art to be used in its fullest sense.… It is the child's process—his thinking, his perceiving, his reaction to his environment that is important."[1] This kind of unrestricted visual expression—the result of an uninterrupted need to communicate—naturally becomes a partner in the creation of a poem.

Illustration ———————————————————————————————————

During the studio's after-school programs in the fall and spring, an art table is set up to serve the students' need to draw and paint as they create their poems. Sometimes a student will first experiment with an idea for a poem through a drawing or painting. Most always the students enjoy illustrating their poems and spend quite a bit of focused time with one or two pictures that resonate with their writing.

These illustrations will most often reiterate aspects of the poems' content in a free and inventive style, thereby reinforcing their meaning. Leah Sutton-Smith's image portraying musical sound waves coming from garden flowers graphically represents her poem *The Song of the Garden* (pp. 70-71). Tess Bogart's warm and kindly apparition visually describes her "special angel": "When thunder scares me, / please smile at me. / When I'm angry / put a flower in my heart" (p. 148). An inventive collage presentation of the night sky serves as a compelling visual companion to Osha Scott's *Jumping on Stars* (pp. 100-101). To illustrate her poem *Reflection,* Maia Castro-Santos provides a beautiful drawing of a young woman looking into a reflecting pool, juxtaposing the deeper, hidden truth of her experience only with the words: "What if there was a whole other world / behind every reflection; / in every pool or mirror, / a whole new place to discover" (pp. 142-143).

At times, the art will help to complete the poem with the use of images to expand necessary details or infuse emotions into the words. The soft lines of Frida Rosner's self-portrait frame a face of mystical intensity that amplifies the power of her poetic vision: "dancing alone under star spangled skies, / will not last forever. / The wind steals a ribbon from my hair / and I leave it here, among the stars" (p. 141). Rosalie Smith's portrait image of her *Aunt Janet* lifts the reader off the page along with Aunt Janet as she ascends from the trampoline. The poem's description is not only punctuated but extended: "Janet, even though your body is old / Your spirit is young and joyful" (pp. 182-183). Ellie Friends elaborates her poetic tribute to a wise old maple by depicting a tree with a hollow trunk that provides shelter for small animals such as squirrels. Compassion, the basis of the tree's wisdom, is thereby visually presented as well—word and image work together to complete the poem (*Wisdom from the Maple,* pp. 62-63). Chloe Rosner personifies a grapevine to give a real-life sense to her poem *Waiting* (pp. 82-83). Likewise, Linaea DiMarino brings her suffering mythological figure to life with an arresting portrait description visually completed with a drawing:

maybe take her hand so her dark
hair will no longer plaster to her red face.

Don't let her cry any more tears of sorrow,
tears of broken glass.

(from *Tears of Broken Glass and Forgotten Gods*, pp. 137-139)

The week-long summer workshops at the *Studio* also provide many opportunities for illustration, with three art tables available and a larger variety of materials as well as stylistic models to use. Examples are drawn from illustrated books such as Eric Carle's marvelous renditions, and the 1890s book and poster movement's Art Nouveau designs, among many others. The students are also encouraged to illustrate short quotes by well-known writers, which provides them with an opportunity to practice the visual interpretation of words. Some of these efforts have been very impressive and have served as examples of the art of illustration for the class (e.g., Isabel McCarthy's illustration of a passage from a Wendell Berry poem, p. 24).

Decoration and Design

Encouraged by young people's love of illustrated books and by their highly acute visual literacy; inspired by an exhibit of illuminated manuscripts from a visit to the Morgan Library and by my own interest in graphic design, several years ago I introduced into the summer sessions a special class on the creation of "beautiful books" in order to showcase the poetry and art created during the week. These books are handcrafted with careful management of the process, which includes gluing the parts of a cover together and sewing in pages. Careful instruction with step-by-step directions is given throughout. Nonetheless, the student creator selects the book paper and waxed thread to use, decorates the cover, creates the title page, and determines the way the poetry and art are displayed on the book's pages. Books have ranged from hard cover folios to signature sewn fold-over paperbacks to hardcover editions with diamond-patterned spines.

Left: Chloe Rosner, *My Poetry Friend*, 2014, handcrafted book—
wrap around, softcover (drawing/illustration)

Right: Chloe Rosner, *Travel Through Poetry*, 2016, handcrafted book—
wrap around, softcover (collage presentation of *Waiting* with illustration)

Left: Ellie Friends, *Whispers of the Wind*, 2013, handcrafted book—
folio, hardcover (collage presentation of *Little Pine*)

Right: Ellie Friends, *If Only*, 2012, handcrafted book—
folio, hardcover (pop-up—illustrated quote: "The Frog does not
drink up the pond/In which he lives." [Native American proverb])

From *Love This Miraculous World*

Wendell Berry

Love this
miraculous world
that we did not make,
that is a gift to us.

Isabel McCarthy, illustration, *Love This Miraculous World* by Wendell Berry

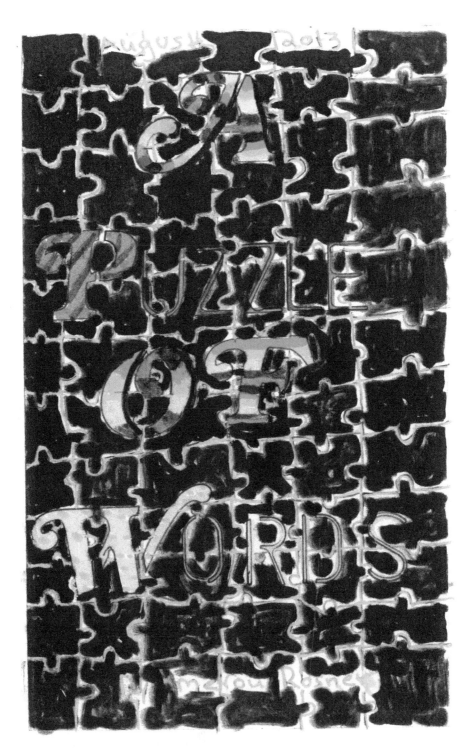

Meroushka Rosner, *A Puzzle of Words*, title page

The book project also affords the opportunity for the invention of decorative and creative applications: border designs that illustrate as well as showcase the poems (Aashna Kinkhabwala, p. 33); broken text with collage applications that exude a kinetic energy and often combine illustration and decoration (Ella Bathory-Peeler, pp. 36-38); combinations of text and imagery to create a new and exciting version of a poem (Isabel McCarthy, p. 106), and title pages of arresting originality displayed throughout *Another World* (e.g., p. 25). The students' books have therefore become more than vessels to hold poems and images; their carefully fabricated covers and pages have been transformed by students into works of art.

Even though the creation of the book's structure is a directed, step-by-step process, students feel very comfortable with the support offered by teachers and fellow students who repeat instructions, help with a task, even thread a needle. It is exciting to witness how the young artists then "work the page"—embellish their poems and illustrations with other applications that are either drawn or pasted into the creative mix. By the final class, urged on by the disco beat of "YMCA," everyone feels a perceptible sense of joy in the fashioning of a beautiful object that not only contains but also contributes to the expression of their work.

Ella Bathory-Peeler sewing her book in The Poetry Studio

Ella Bathory-Peeler, *Hear Our Voices,* book page

References

1   Viktor Lowenfeld and W. Lambert Brittain, *Creative and Mental Growth* (New York: Macmillan, 1975), 8-9.

Poetry and Art by Young People

Evil Versus Love

Poetry is like love armies
that hold off the dark.

If poetry is locked
in a dark trap,
the world will turn black.

Poetry threatens Evil
with weapons
of happiness,
soldiers of love.

Poetry's wisdom wins the battle.

SAMUEL GARBARINO
Written at age 7

CHAPTER ONE

Journeys & Transformations

Finding Home

Pencil hovering over paper,
unsure of what to write,
who to become,

what to bring to life –

whose story?
The chipmunk, the horse,
the man with the lame foot?
Or the girl who doesn't know herself.
It spins a tale of magic places
and long journeys and hard work
about a girl trying to find herself.
She travels far and wide,
asks questions to the trees,
the animals, the sky.
They all say she knows,
she just has to remember.
And at the end of the tale,

she knows –

the girl with the
pencil hovering over the paper.

Grow with Me

Grow with me
and we will watch each other's faces grow wrinkles.
Grow with me
and we will snap our fingers and hum at the fireside.
We'll dance and sing like *kachinas* at the parties and festivals.
Tell jokes when we hike and laugh in the tent.
Make up stories and share them with our friends and families.
So grow with me,
spend your life with mine,
and we'll sit as mountains, hand in hand,
the ocean lapping at our feet
like old turtles meditating until dawn.

CLAIRE HOLMES
Written at age 9

Silence

Gentle silence,
the chaos of unchecked certainty
in its wildest form.
The dream of the dark,
the melody of light.
The charismatic pause,
so fleeting, so swift
it echoes for miles,
for years, for seconds.
It tempers the rampaged spirit,
and enrages the steadiest heart.
Silence, the most fragile gift,
yet the one most abused.
It is the baseline of all.

GRACE MARTENSON
Written at age 15

Ella Bathory-Peeler,
Full Time Cartographer,
written at age 16;
book pages

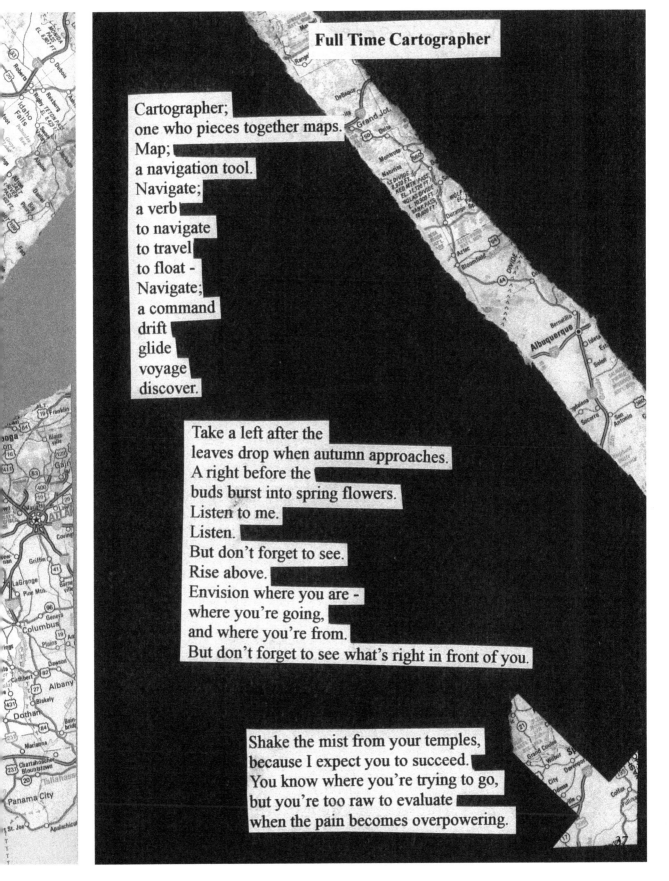

Full Time Cartographer

Cartographer;
one who pieces together maps.
Map;
a navigation tool.
Navigate;
a verb
to navigate
to travel
to float -
Navigate;
a command
drift
glide
voyage
discover.

Take a left after the
leaves drop when autumn approaches.
A right before the
buds burst into spring flowers.
Listen to me.
Listen.
But don't forget to see.
Rise above.
Envision where you are -
where you're going,
and where you're from.
But don't forget to see what's right in front of you.

Shake the mist from your temples,
because I expect you to succeed.
You know where you're trying to go,
but you're too raw to evaluate
when the pain becomes overpowering.

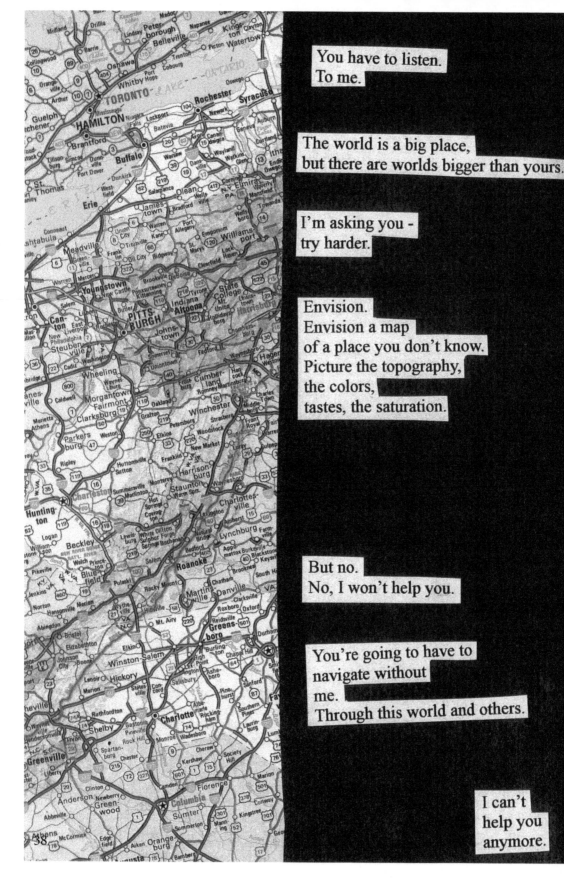

You have to listen.
To me.

The world is a big place,
but there are worlds bigger than yours.

I'm asking you -
try harder.

Envision.
Envision a map
of a place you don't know.
Picture the topography,
the colors,
tastes, the saturation.

But no.
No, I won't help you.

You're going to have to
navigate without
me.
Through this world and others.

I can't
help you
anymore.

I dared to carry the weight of the world
on my shoulders.

To become the becoming.
To roll in the rolling waves of chance.
To love with my heart wide open.
To play with my spirit animal.
To dream of my wildest hope.
I dared to live.

LILY CHARKEY-BUREN
Written at age 10

Galaxy of Stars

I am a twig, and I am sitting
and singing to myself.
I am a river, and I make
the stillest flow of music.
I am a leaf flowing through the wind
like a shade of sunlight through a tree.
I am a flower, and I am flowing
with the noise of cool rain.
I am the world in a galaxy of stars,
stars that sing into my heart.

SAMUEL GARBARINO
Written at age 9

Exploring Myself

Don't be afraid.

You're not allowed to hide.

In the end, you have no choice;

you will have to meet me.

Some day, you might even know me.

But eventually, you will have to understand me —

maybe even embrace me.

It is inevitable.

It will happen.

Because I am you —

the other side of you.

What is this?

How are you me?

I am the part of you left in nature:

the tree you climbed,

the flower you planted,

the path you left.

Will you follow me back to myself?

AASHNA KINKHABWALA
Written at age 15

Chloe Rosner, *Turning Back*

Turning Back

Almost. I almost left.
I couldn't though.
It was too hard.
Too sorrowful.
I always hated goodbyes,
and leaving was too much for my heart to take.
I wouldn't leave my home,
even if it was just for the cold months.
I could not leave my oak tree,
my wonderful oak tree,
so tall, so full of food,
so cheery and grand.
Instead I stayed,
warm and cozy in my nest,
curled up, head under wings.
And the others left without me.
Only me
in my loving nest
beneath my loving oak.

CHLOE ROSNER
Written at age 9

43

When Summer Left

How did summer leave?

How did it slip away, without me noticing?

Did it slowly dwindle, one day at a time,

till the last drop disappeared,

like a puddle drying up?

Did it speed by, in the moments

when my eyes were closed,

like a hummingbird

too precious to stay long?

Did it just drift along,

like a lazy river,

leaving days behind it?

How did summer leave?

Where did the summer fly to?

Did it fly to the same place

as unheard sounds

and untraveled paths,

a lonely place to wait?

Did it vacation

to some other land,

carried by its own warm breezes?

Did it settle into memory,

napping the winter away?

Where did the summer fly to?

When did the summer go?

Did it slip behind a tree

when a thought

of cold water became a shiver?

Did it scamper away

when it saw an extra quilt?

Did it notice the swallows

spreading rumors of autumn?

Where did the summer go?

Who did the summer say goodbye to?

Did summer know

that when it comes back

there will be new fingers

pulling its green grass,

new toes digging into

its sun warmed beaches?

Did it realize

that bent backs and

wrinkled hands

that had rejoiced at its

gentle days

will not do so when it returns?

Did it hear

that those children it loved

will have changed,

grown?

Who did summer say goodbye to?

What does summer hope for?

Does it hope to see

less people,

more space for its green grasses, when it returns?

Does it hope to see

more people,

each new person a promise?

Did it want to leave?

Does it want to return?

What does summer hope for?

Why did summer disappear?

Did it leave so it

could return,

refreshed,

like a jump into water?

Did it need space,

time to rejuvenate,

or was it just making room

for something new?

Why did summer disappear?

Erin LeBlanc
Written at age 12

My Stone Path

The flat stones are so far apart
I have to leap from one to another.
It is difficult,
but I enjoy it.
I enjoy the time that I have
in the air between the stones,
before my feet hit the future,
but after they have left the past.
This in-between stage is my time to change.
It's the moment I have to switch feet,
so I can land on the next stone
slightly differently,
putting challenge into my leaping life.

ELLA BATHORY-PEELER
Written at age 13

Ella Bathory-Peeler, *My Stone Path*

Invocation

Closed bud of the hibiscus —

how we yearn

for you to open.

Show your face,

radiating your beauty.

Join the chorus of the other flowers

who are waiting for your return.

Closed bud of the hibiscus,

do you remember last summer

as you danced with the daisies

after coming out of a deep dream

Do you remember the poets,

being their inspiration?

Come back; remind us

of the beauty and love

left in the world.

Let us behold

your scarlet petals,

rippled,

like a pond

after a stone is thrown in.

ZOLA VON KRUSENSTIERN
Written at age 12

He tried to find his friend.

He thought he only needed to search

long enough to find him.

But his friend wasn't there.

As if he was gazing

in his friend's mirror —

foggy, shifted.

He looked and smelled the same,

he even spoke the same.

But he wasn't there.

Gone, changed,

nothing he remembered.

EZRA MARDER
Written at age 13

Transfiguration

A small hill becomes a mountain.

A weed is a tree.

A pond is the Pacific.

The moss is grass, so green.

An ant transforms to a human.

A spider, a monster — huge!

The sacred breaths we take

become the wind

that travels far and wide.

LEAH SUTTON-SMITH
Written at age 10

Leah Sutton-Smith, *Transfiguration*

Beautiful

Beautiful.
like the dress she would wear
Christmas night, red and green and white
and the lipstick she would wear to
make her look all right, red, silver and bright.
Beautiful.
like the shoes she broke when
she ran to have fun with just a
couple of friends,
high on hope, she was thoughtless,
full of laughter, always laughing,
dancing till dawn,
father angry.
Beautiful.
like her heart, the one she would
give away too often, a
heart half gone, yet fully open;
her heart a painting, a thousand little mistakes
made into something amazing.
She is art, her arms the paintbrushes,
her body the canvas.
Beautiful.
like her ears, she promised
to listen, to listen to herself more often.
She heard it all, everything she wanted to hear.

She *promised* to hear, ears wide open.
Beautiful,
she told herself when down and under
the weather, makeup smeared, paintings ruined.
"Beautiful,"
she said aloud,
and vowed to get better.

EMMA SPRENGER
Written at age 14

CHAPTER TWO

Nature as Teacher

& Nature as Metaphor

Grace Martenson, book page

The Emotion Tree

Emotions are like the rings of a tree,
one inside the other,
working together
to create one's soul.
They build upon one another.
Each, simple component
joining together.
Even the negative emotions are important:
anger,
fear,
anxiety.
Without these emotions, your trunk will start to
shrink.
The absence of these rings will make you,
as a person,
less interesting.
If you are open to new emotions and let them come
as you grow,
your emotion tree will thrive,
your trunk will broaden,
your branches will extend towards the sky.
Each emotion,
even if you think you could do without it,
makes up
who you are.

ELLA BATHORY-PEELER
Written at age 14

Little Pine

Little pine,
embracing her stone slope —
little pine,
standing proud in the shadows
of her tall neighbors —
little pine,
shielding the spider's fragile nest
from the reckless wind —

teach me to love the stone
that blocks my path;
teach me to stand
even when cast into darkness;
teach me to protect the spider
unconditionally
and ask for nothing in return.

ELLIE FRIENDS
Written at age 13

Big Frog

Big frog in a small pond.
Big frog, so still,
as still as a stone.
Amber eyes stare into my soul.
Big frog, I'm not like you —
you sit in meditation
while I am always rushing,
rushing through life.
Big frog, wise king of the pond,
bring me calm and peace,
so I can walk through life,
stop seeing in black and white,
unlock the cage I'm trapped in.

Ava Rosenzweig-Davidovits
Written at age 11

Sunny Afternoon

The succulent quivers in a nonchalant hello,

I sit,   sipping sun

and words of warmth and sunshine

tremble on the tip of my pencil.

The succulent, invariably envious,

casts a shadow across my words,

to remind me   of all that exists

in the absence of the sun.

The Sun's Path

The sun is like a morning glory
opening up,

saying good morning to the day.

The sun picks its way carefully,

moving at a slow pace

like a lady in a gown of golden light.

The sun has diamonds falling in its
wake

as it travels toward dusk.

The sun is warm as it sets,

setting off an array of vibrant colors.

The sun disappears into the night,

but never sleeps,

always ready to wake

someone else's slumber.

Luna Weiss
Written at age 11

Frida Rosner, *Sunny Afternoon*, written at age 15; book page

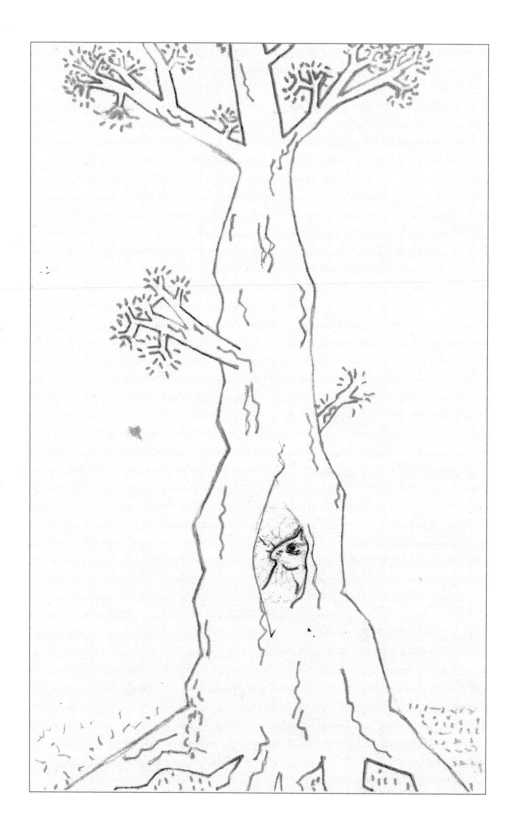

Wisdom from the Maple

The maple murmurs
fables from a time
long ago,
her voice a clear mountain stream.

Listen, she tells me.

Listen to the stones
all piled together
as they chant
to the forest.

Listen to the sun
as her sweet tendrils
of warmth
envelop you.

Listen to the beating
in your chest
let it seep away
and fill every corner
that has ever been
with love.

ELLIE FRIENDS
Written at age 14

Ellie Friends, *Wisdom from the Maple*

Wise Evergreen

Today, I heard the evergreen calling to me.
In a deep voice, he whispered:
"Come closer,
 come hear my wise secrets.
Remember today, to be kind,
 generous and respectful
to all others."
His wisdom drifts into my spirit
like autumn leaves in the breeze.
Today, the evergreen taught me
to understand kindness.

ELLIE JELLEMA-HARTER
Written at age 8

Ellie Jellema-Harter, *Wise Evergreen*

65

Late Gratitude

The maple didn't appreciate what she had
until it was gone.

She didn't welcome the child's companionship
until it was too late.

She thought she disliked the rope swing
and the child that went with it, hanging from her wrist,
until the rope and the joy
disappeared.

She wished she had relaxed,
watching the boy dance around her
snatching leaves from the air.

She wished she had laughed,
tossing the boy playfully back and forth.

She wished she had loved the boy,
and had told him how she felt.

If only she had found
her heart in time.

ELLA BATHORY-PEELER
Written at age 15

Joe Pye Weed

Look at them,
the butterflies
dancing from flower to flower.
They remind me of my past,
hopping from then to now.
They mentor me.

Look at them,
sure about tomorrow.
Shall it rain?
Their wings open up to the world
as I would love to open up to myself.

Look at them,
they tell me to relax
and breathe
and think
and float upon my path.

Look at them,
smiling under the sun
telling me to do the same.

Look at them,
my mentors.

EMMA SPRENGER
Written at age 12

CHAPTER THREE

Nature Characters & Conversations with Nature

The Song of the Garden

The beautiful, maroon hibiscus
opens her face to the rain,
singing for joy
in the foggy garden,
with raindrops on every petal.
Her elegant, rolling voice
quivers in the air,
reverberating around the meadow.
Her pink sister hibiscus
joins her in high-pitched harmony,
a contrasting blend.
The hostas' lavender bagpipes
twine in and out,
in and out of the tune.

The nasturtiums,
the black-eyed Susans,
the daisies add their chords,
intoning: "oh joy, oh joy."
Every flower,
every leaf,
every petal in the garden
add their vibrating voices,
singing the song of the garden.

LEAH SUTTON-SMITH
Written at age 11

Leah Sutton-Smith, *The Song of the Garden*

The Day Lily Whispers...

A Book of Poetry
By: Maia

August, 2014

Maia Castro-Santos, *The Day Lily Whispers*, title page

Listen to the Willow's Words

Listen to the sound of the wind
weaving in and out of my long arms.
Listen to the sun tinkling
like soft, gentle bells.
Listen to the orchestra of crickets
playing in the ferns.
Listen to the lilies singing
their joyous song.
Listen to the family of black-eyed Susans
sharing their secrets with the maple.
Listen to the apple tree
whispering its wisdom to the stone wall.
Listen to the shadows
shifting their positions.
Listen to the garden
full of music and laughter.
Listen to the frogs,
their deep voices
singing along
to the sweet melody of nature.

HILLARY LEEDS
Written at age 9

Connection

The willow is unique
in its own way.
Its branches spread wide,
swaying in the sunlit breeze.
The sun, a chandelier
blazing on the slender, long leaves.

Willow, your heart
is a glorious jewel.
There is only one rope
on this planet
that connects
you and me.

Luna Weiss
Written at age 8

Luna Weiss, *Connection*

75

Zinnia

Like so many children,
Zinnia would listen
for the opportunity to shine.
Days fade into night,
but still Zinnia waits.
Silver moonlight
spills from the sky,
lifting the heads of many,
but not hers.
Still, she waits.
Sisters bloom
into radiant flowers,
but Zinnia's eyes
see nothing but earth.
The sun comes and goes,
but only the stars' velvet touch
can reach her drooping leaves
and solemn expression.

One night,

when the stars are shining,

the memory of nothingness
fades

and in its place

is the urge to bloom.

CHLOE ROSNER
Written at age 10

Rose

She used to be perfect,

not a blemish on her blooming skin.

She used to stand straight,

wearing a crown of sweet perfume.

Children's laughter tickled her ears,

and she would sing along with the crickets.

Now her head is starting to droop,

her petals folding like faded washcloths,

the stem that held her beginning to bend.

But on warm nights, she still remembers

the voices of nature praising her

as she danced to evening birdsong.

CLAIRE HOLMES
Written at age 12

Long ago I was a daffodil
bursting from the misty earth.
My buttery-yellow petals shone
beneath hundreds of stars.
Long ago my joyful spirit
kissed a girl's hand.
Her heart dazzled.
Long ago I, the daffodil, sang a
song of poetry.

Tess Bogart
Written at age 11

Lily Charkey-Buren, *Celosia*

Celosia[*]

In the garden

Celosia stands still and tall

waiting for someone to question her status

but no one does.

Her hair, purple as an everlasting sunset

and as lively as snakes.

Her eyes, ice-cold daggers gleaming with glee.

Celosia keeps her sadness bottled up,

never to be seen.

Her presence is daring and strong.

When she walks, she takes bold steps,

not itty-bitty steps, never lingering a moment too long.

Her heart, sweet and kind,

but the world is blind to her.

They only see the tough shell hiding her spirit.

Celosia, a young 12 year old

but everyone thinks she is older.

She shares her presence with everyone

but leaves when her time is up

like a hummingbird pausing for just enough time.

That is the mystical life of Celosia.

LILY CHARKEY-BUREN
Written at age 10   [*]A garden flower

Waiting

Grapevine is an old man,
shoulders hunched over,
wrinkled fingers reaching out,
hoping one day
to grasp a young cloud.
The old man hums
to himself as he waits.
He hums a slow
and steady tune,
dawn to dusk.
He still waits
this very day.

Chloe Rosner
Written at age 8

Chloe Rosner, *Waiting*

An Orchestra of Nature

The smallest things have the most to say —
one blade of grass,
a bumblebee,
a single leaf of the maple tree,
one silky white petal of a flower,
the black and orange butterfly
that I keep on seeing,
that one clump of moss,
a single pine needle —
everything making a different sound,
an orchestra of nature.
You need everything
to make a perfect world,
as you need every note
to make a perfect song;
every little thing is important.

ELLIE JELLEMA-HARTER
Written at age 10

To Talk and to Speak

Trees like to speak
with the wave of their leaves,
like fingertips moving
slower and faster,
working with the wind,
tilting each leaf,
waving their branches,
sending their tree-signals
to each other
through each other,
speaking
with the wind.

I like to speak
with a nod of my head,
with a smile, with a frown,
with an echoing laugh,
though no human speaking,
whether it be out loud
or with silent signals
is as beautiful
as
the trees.

ISABEL MCCARTHY
Written at age 12

Listen

Listen to the wind —
its breath spreads out
over the world like wings and soars
brushing the tree tops —
I hear strength.

FIONA TIERNEY
Written at age 11

Listen to the sun —
it beats down on the earth
making the leaves dance,
the sun beats to the songs of life —
I hear rhythm.

Listen to the rain,
showering down, screaming as it falls
from the sky, afraid —
I hear fear.

Listen to the flowers,
nestled up close with their brothers and sisters,
chattering and laughing —
I hear love.

If you just pause and listen to the world's music
you might be surprised what you can hear.

Fiona Tierney, *Listen*

Sounds of Nature

The leaves in the wind
sound like maracas,
a constant beat
in the forest.
Moss speaks to me,
only me,
in a voice as soft
as strumming strings
of the harp.
The ferns sound
like the rattling tail
of a rattlesnake.
The sun laughs
as all the voices of the forest
make a peaceful chorus.

ROWAN MUZZY
Written at age 9

Tadpole, you are my brother.
Your body as tiny
as the moon of my fingernail,
your legs scrunched together
like a broken spiderweb,
your head pointed
like an arrow,
your tail as squiggly
as a worm.
Tadpole, you fascinate me.

Silas Muzzy
Written at age 8

Siberian Elm

thousand-fingered hands
rejoice as the low-flung clouds
grace the outstretched leaves.

Rhys McGovern, *Siberian Elm*, written and illustrated at age 16; book page

Secrets

The way to the forest's heart
is not through a trail
that interrupts
the drowsy murmur
of the ferns.
The secret of the forest's heart
can never be told on a map.
It is ever changing.
It whirls and loops
through sun-dappled glades,
laced with spiderwebs.
It dances on tiptoes
across giggling brooks
where the sun
splashes among
the pebbles.
The secret of the forest
lies within us all,
and sometimes,
in finding it,
we find ourselves.

ELLIE OLIVER
Written at age 14

CHAPTER FOUR

Stretching Borders

Frida Rosner, book and quill

A Mistake of the Wise Man

The wise man was wrong.

The crack in my heart only grew.

The place in between is a city of sadness,

an oasis of happy memories dissolving

      in a pool of my tears.

Frida Rosner
Written at age 12

The Girl from the River

She stands there,
up to her ankles,
letting the river rush
over her feet.
I've heard stories
of how she got there —
but never the same one twice.
Some say her whole family drowned,
others say she ran away from home,
but today as I watch her
in her blue jean overalls
and sun-bleached hair
dancing in the wind,
she looks so peaceful
and, for a second,
I'm jealous
of the girl from the river.

WILLA REDDEN
Written at age 13

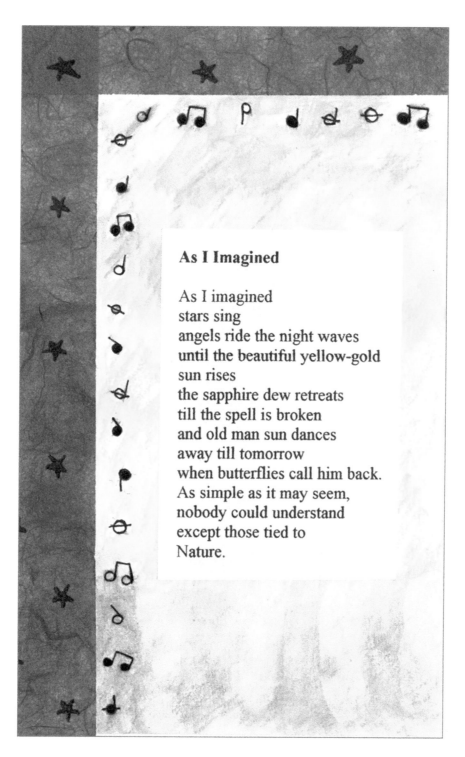

As I Imagined

As I imagined
stars sing
angels ride the night waves
until the beautiful yellow-gold
sun rises
the sapphire dew retreats
till the spell is broken
and old man sun dances
away till tomorrow
when butterflies call him back.
As simple as it may seem,
nobody could understand
except those tied to
Nature.

Aashna Kinkhabwala, *As I Imagined*, written at age 14; book page

Blossoming Words

What if every flower bloomed a word?

What if each stalk was a sentence?

What would you hear with your eyes?

What if each flower does bloom a word?

A word carried in its heart,

a word we can hear, not see,

a word that we maybe imagine,

but was always meant to be.

The Rose of Sharon would blossom

not in petals,

but in delicious dreamy words —

fanciful,

graceful,

and *delight*

would grace its stalk

which would speak in sentences of beauty.

The leaves might whisper

pastel sunsets,

rippling lakes

and *full moons.*

Hydrangeas would bloom in clusters of letters

forming words like

secret,

peace

and *promise.*

Black-eyed Susans
would laugh, singing words
joy,
welcome,
and *happy ending.*
The Hibiscus would grandly display words of a queen
importance,
perfection,
glory.
The garden would be bursting
with words,
words that tickle the tongue,
words sweet like a summer evening
words that blossomed.
Words meant to fill a garden,
words that were always there,
waiting for a listener.

Erin LeBlanc
Written at age 12

Osha Scott, *Jumping on Stars*

Jumping on Stars

In your dreams
if you truly believe,
you can fly up to the sparkling starry sky.
You can travel through the night air,
jumping on the little glowing stars
like stepping stones across the deep blue creek.
You might hear singing and splashing
from the water spirits.
Then you slowly drop with weariness
and fall into your warm fluffy bed.
You will remember the moon's big, kind
eyes watching over you.

OSHA SCOTT
Written at age 10

The Girl Who Painted the Autumn Leaves

There is a girl,
her dress, the color of autumn leaves,
her hair, as brown
as soil after it rains,
her eyes twinkling
like stars.
She has a paintbrush
that spreads color over the earth.
Her heart filled with colors —
vibrant red, a dazzling yellow,
and a sparkling orange.
The girl who painted autumn leaves.

MENA EICHELBERGER
Written at age 8

Mena Eichelberger, *The Girl Who Painted Autumn Leaves*

Maise Sperling, *God's Eye*

God's Eye

I took a walk,

wanting to see the moon.

But when I looked at the moon,

I saw god's eye watching me,

a dark god.

I hesitated,

then gazed at the dark night sky.

A shiver of fear crept down my body.

I felt that the moon was going to shatter.

A black tear flickered down my face

like a shooting star.

The fear stayed in my heart

like a rock.

MAISE SPERLING
Written at age 9

Pinocchio

Words pour carelessly
from your mouth
like water
from a teapot
labeled "tea"
but I can see
that your nose
is in another galaxy.

Isabel McCarthy, *Pinocchio*, written at age 14; book page

An Ominous Orange

Shadows stretched across the hillside
like long purple bruises
in an ochre sky;
the wind was dancing so fast
that the leaves buzzed and whirred.

In the commotion
the horizon reached up to devour the sun,
but it left a ragged hole
and a sudden stillness
that silenced even the trees.

Frida Rosner
Written at age 15

If I Could Paint
a New World

If I could paint a new place in the sea
If I could dive into my painting of the sea,
I'd ride the back of a blue whale,
a whale carrying me around the world
like a ferry boat.

If I could dive into my painting of the sea,
I'd watch a lighthouse flashing magnificent colors.

While the moon slips out from behind clouds,
      the whale leaves me
as a big wave washes me back out of my painting.

ROWAN SCOTT
Written at age 8

Rowan Scott, *If I Could Paint a New World*

Sam Bogart, *Death*

Death

Death, you come and go
like the colors of the leaves.
Your heart, inky black
like life after the apocalypse.
Death, why come to us?
Why greet us in a hostile way?
Why take us one by one?
Death, don't take me.

SAM BOGART
Written at age 11

Tree of Life

The tree
of Life
cherishes each
thing from our
existence to a speck
of dust.
Each branch
holds a secret just
waiting to be
found.
She cradles
the colors
and uses
the earth
as a canvas.
In summer the flowers
bloom on her branches.
In autumn one secret
falls with her leaves.
In winter she
appears regal and thoughtful.
In spring her trunk is
one with the rain.

Her roots planted in the
garden of
immortality reach
down in the mud
pushing away the clumps
of hatred.
The universe is her
blanket, stitched with the
white of compassion and
the pink of peace.
Good Night.

Naneh Pittman
Written at age 10

112

Dizzying Melodies

The crack in the sidewalk sings to the sky
until my head spins
and the sky switches place with the ground,
and back again.

My memories come apart at the seams,
unraveling.
A moth-eaten moment disappears as a stain sets in.

My imagination acts as my luminary,
there to light my way,
though I'll admit to my apprehension
for the time of an eclipse,
one day.

FRIDA ROSNER
Written at age 13

Singing

When I'm feeling down,
I sing,
my whole body sings.

My sadness blows away
like dust in the wind.

I sing my favorite songs
over and over
until they enter my heart.

My songs drift
from my room
to a magical garden.

My songs open the flowers' petals
as they reach for a bright summer sun.
Oh singing
you are my guardian spirit.

Tess Bogart
Written at age 12

Baseball

When the world is pounding
      in my ears,
I see a boy diving for a ball,
diving like a falcon
cutting through a sunset sky.

The boy catches the ball mid-air,
all thoughts are washed away.
All worries are swallowed into
darkness, into a forgotten land.

When the boy stops,
his worries float up like mist.
When the boy sprints across the summer field,
it's as though the wings of an eagle
engulf his body,
engulf his heart.

SAM BOGART
Written at age 11

CHAPTER FIVE

Animal Magic
& Magical Creatures

How I Became Myself

Before the earth was born,
before I became myself
I was the Bird of Beauty and Health.
I had a fawn's head,
a hummingbird's body,
a peacock's tail.
I brought a cure,
a cure of love,
a cure that could help any sickness
no matter how dangerous.
I was the only one of my kind.
I made my voice loud and said:
"To those who are lonely and afraid,
there's always a part of you
that's leaping with joy.
Come with me,
I'll show you."
That's how I became the girl I am today.

Lila Blau
Written at age 8

Grace Martenson, book title page

119

Lion Cub

I was born a lion cub,
curiosity in my spirit.
My eyes darted
from one direction to another,
wondering.
My ears were so magical
they could hear
the whisper of flowers,
the gentle voice of a single leaf
trembling on the oak.
I was born with pride,
my body never knew sorrow.

ROSALIE SMITH
Written at age 10

Rosalie Smith, *Lion Cub*

I am The Bird That Flutters Against Your Window in The Morning

I am the bird that helps you
    through your despair.
As the wind blows I am there
    to ease you into rising from your
    crippled dreams.
Morning is over.
    Now you have forgotten your
    nightmares.
The interchangeable day goes on.
High in the sky you can see me
    watching
    waiting
    waiting for you to call me,
    call me to your aid.
Even you know that I will one
    day evaporate into nothing but
    your dreams
    dreams of beautiful days
    beautiful days to make you
    happy.

But you still wait
    wait for the perfect time
    to call me.

I am the bird that sounds like
    no other
    looks like the sun so bright
you can see me from miles
    away.
Rise that Tuesday morning
    but let me wake you
    wake you for the last time.
Darkness will disappear.

Meroushka Rosner
Written at age 10

Wise Porcupine

I shuffle at my own pace
like the porcupine,
waddling, doing my own thing.
Others misunderstand me.
Others don't see the
curiosity in my eyes.
Others don't feel my
good nature.
Others don't recognize
how wonder lives in my soul.

I, the Wise One,
know how to ward off
those who don't understand me.
My inside quills
are the knowledge of
keeping distance,
of knowing that solitude
is my home.

CHLOE HULL
Written at age 13

The Day I Cut the Sun

The sound of my wings
match my heartbeat exactly.
The song I sing, forever lingers
  in my soul.
I soar through the morning sunrise
almost splitting it in two.
The elderly hawks scold me for breaking the sun,
but I'm not listening,
a bright red maple leaf has caught my attention.
I no longer remember the sun
and its cut or the hawks,
my mind is set on catching that leaf.
Faster faster weaving in and out of the trees.
My heart is no longer in sync with my wings.
It is thumping too rapidly for them to keep up.
Few minutes later, I'm perched on a branch
out of breath but happy,
the leaf clutched in my beak.
Satisfied, I look at the sun,
expecting a congratulation on my work
but instead it weeps over its light gash,
the same color as my leaf, blood red.

CHLOE ROSNER
Written at age 9

124

Chloe Rosner, *The Day I Cut the Sun*

My heart is an owl.

My heart is flying out of my body,

rising up to the full moon

that glows

like a million fireflies.

My heart is an owl —

"who-who-who — "

in the middle of the night,

as dark

as a house

with no lights on,

my voice

as soft

as a cricket singing.

MAISE SPERLING
Written at age 6

Sensation

Exhilarating tranquility,
a wild openness
it takes me over.
My thoughts are irrelevant
the human within me is absent.
The chase begins.

My feet are like heartbeats on the ground.
There is only silence in my ears.
My instincts have taken the reins
they lead me through a maze
of branches and thorns.

When I stand still,
my human returns.
My ears fill with the sounds of the forest
the wild within fades.
A sorrow swells inside me.

I whisper a promise
I know I won't break.
"I will return."

GRACE MARTENSON
Written at age 14

Maise Sperling, *Secret Gathering*

Secret Gathering

I believe I can hear the animals speaking.

I believe the animals are having a secret gathering
away
from darkness,
meanness,
hate.

I believe the animals are whispering to each other
like the wind chiming to the rhythm of words.

My heart is beating to the voices of animals.

I believe I will hear them once again.

MAISE SPERLING
Written at age 9

Never Without You

Last November, I saw my doubt in a wolf's body.

He turned his head sharply,

eyes an icy blue

and thick, gray fur, soft like wings.

Then he ducked under the trees,

tail nodding in the wind.

But I still see him dawdling

in the throat of my mind.

CLAIRE HOLMES
Written at age 12

CHAPTER SIX

Mythical Worlds
& Mythic Beings

Chloe Rosner,
*Into the Purple
Mist*, title page

The Girl Whose Heart Rose into the Sun

Long ago
the sun was dim and dark,
faded and gray.

Long ago
the birds did not sing of light
and spring blossoms
but sang of discomfort and
unforgivable deeds.

But there was a girl who believed
in the sun's reign.
Her belief like a ship anchored
to the sea of her soul.

Her heart, so illuminated,
rose up into the sky

and instead of a cloak of darkness,
a tapestry of Love
woven from her fingertips
formed into the sun.

Now the birds sing of light
and spring blossoms.
Now instead of dark and dim,
the sun hovers
filled with Beauty.

MAISE SPERLING
Written at age 11

The Figure in The Mist

You can never see her,

never hear her,

only sense her,

The Figure in The Mist.

Long long ago

she made a sacrifice,

a vow,

breaking her bodily ties.

She now lies shrouded,

shrouded in the dark stormy mists of time.

Guarding the world,

watching every child,

every young man and woman,

every old man or woman,

every human on Earth.

You can sometimes see an eye,

the hand of a child,

a tiny flash of colorless hair.

The Figure in the Mist.

The Figure watching everyone on Earth,

forever.

FIONA GOODMAN
Written at age 10

Fiona Goodman, *The Figure in the Mist*

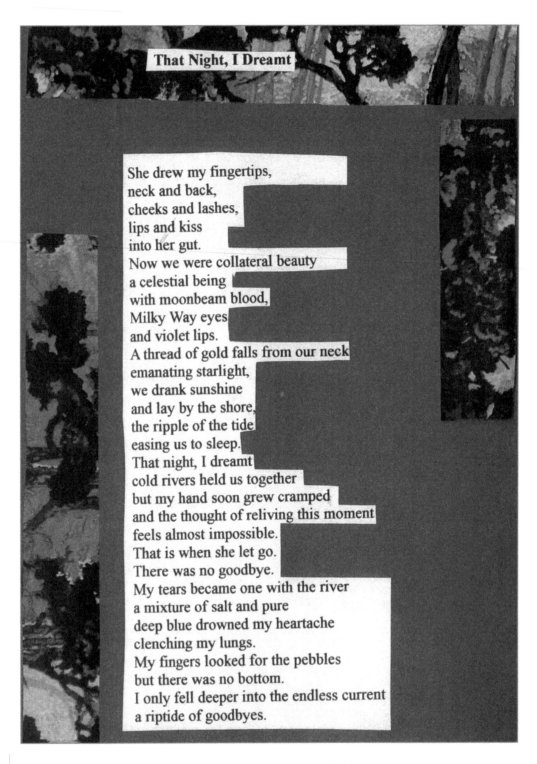

That Night, I Dreamt

She drew my fingertips,
neck and back,
cheeks and lashes,
lips and kiss
into her gut.
Now we were collateral beauty
a celestial being
with moonbeam blood,
Milky Way eyes
and violet lips.
A thread of gold falls from our neck
emanating starlight,
we drank sunshine
and lay by the shore,
the ripple of the tide
easing us to sleep.
That night, I dreamt
cold rivers held us together
but my hand soon grew cramped
and the thought of reliving this moment
feels almost impossible.
That is when she let go.
There was no goodbye.
My tears became one with the river
a mixture of salt and pure
deep blue drowned my heartache
clenching my lungs.
My fingers looked for the pebbles
but there was no bottom.
I only fell deeper into the endless current
a riptide of goodbyes.

Tae Weiss, *That Night I Dreamt*, written at age 14; book page

Tears of Broken Glass and Forgotten Gods

It's hard to remember her on days like this
when the sun shines bright and breezes caress you.

For she is in a dark place and has been so for a long time,
a place where the mold and mildew claw their
way over the stone in a war to survive.

This is where she sits crying glistening tears
of sorrow, pain and broken glass.

She sits on a seat of bones and burned books
with broken dreams and hopes surrounding her chair,

they come in different forms: cracked and
severed links of jewelry,

shattered vases and sculpture, arts of unequal
beauty never to be whole,
lost forgotten puzzle pieces gray with
age, never to see their homes,

clear and colored glass in which hopeful
eyes gazed through or gave celebration never to be used,
just lie there shattered.

Linaea DiMarino, *Tears of Broken Glass and Forgotten Gods*

She didn't always sit here, she used to have
a name lost in all the pain.

She was young with the world, enjoying
the sun with her family, but then they gave her a job,

while they rose as gods she was left forgotten
to care for the memories of those pushed away,

the whipped ones whose blood drowned the earth,

the ones pushed from high places to lay
shattered like the fragments around her chair,

pushed from their community for no reason.

The world grew to hate them and
she must hold on to that,

so send a little love her way
so she won't sit with memories of hell, fire and greed.

Maybe then she can step into the sun and
away from that sorrowful place of rock and stone,

maybe take her hand so her dark
hair will no longer plaster to her red face.

Don't let her cry any more tears of sorrow,
tears of broken glass.

Linaea DiMarino
Written at age 13

Heaven

Sorrow is blue,
sorrow is the rain falling from the sky.
Two souls
that used to be brothers
now shadowed ghosts
walking slowly, silent.
A light pink tree in a field
giving peace and happiness
and life.
Two ghosts change
into white spirits
and sit there —
flowers bloom around them.

ALBAN NEIL
Written at age 8

Dark circles reside beneath my tired eyes

but I continue to dance,

and my partner is the moon.

But the music of the crickets is nostalgic,

and I know this summer of late nights, dancing alone

      under star spangled skies,

will not last forever.

The wind steals a ribbon from my hair

and I leave it here, among the stars.

FRIDA ROSNER
Written at age 13

Frida Rosner, self portrait

Reflection

I hear voices softly singing
as I look into the pond.
I see the reflections of trees and flowers;
I see the reflection of myself.
The wavering images dance and twinkle,
as sunlight strokes the water.
The reflections keep singing,
beckoning me closer,
inviting me into their realm.
What if there was a whole other world
behind every reflection;
in every pool or mirror,
a whole new place to discover.
The reflections sing:
"come closer, come closer!"
and I reach out my hand to enter their world,
but as my finger touches the smooth surface,
the silvery ripple shatters the image,
and the reflection is gone.
The song is gone.

MAIA CASTRO-SANTOS
Written at age 12

Maia Castro-Santos, *Reflection*

Jolie Tate-Giordano, *Water Fairy*

Water Fairy

In the cradle
of a lotus flower,
a fairy whispered to me:
"wake up, fairy girl —
come walk on the
pond's water with me.
Let your bare feet
touch the cool water,
gentle like a fox's fur."
We walked together,
magic in our souls.

Jolie Tate-Giordano
Written at age 9

Stars of Silver

I call to the stars.

I long for your dust of love and peace.

I long for your silver drops and beams of light,

light of the gods,

the gods that make the earth spin round,

and the gods that make seasons

and snow, flowers, leaves that fall.

Silver stars, give me a better world.

MADISON DIMARINO
Written at age 10

Madison DiMarino, *Stars of Silver*

Tess Bogart, *Untitled*: "Oh special angel…"

Oh special angel
will you be my guardian spirit?
When I'm lonely
will you put happiness inside me?
When I'm sad
will you hug me
with your silvery wings?
When thunder scares me,
please smile at me.
When I'm angry,
put a flower in my heart.

TESS BOGART
Written at age 8

Daughter of the Milky Way

They say my dark side
overcame me, that my thoughts
for the world are bitter and cold.
They say I'm the darkest at night,
but at night my love shines purest.
At night I run through sacred fields of ancestors,
befriend the stars before they burst
at dawn, we sing to each other songs
of ancient memories.
At twilight I sit
on the Big Dipper, my long
raven hair is blown
by the wind to create
the shadow that will cause
the night to begin.

MAISE SPERLING
Written at age 12

The Twilight Princess

Have you ever wondered what lies between and under?

Have you ever wondered what slips through
  the dark to scare or comfort you?

Have you ever wondered who paints
  the sky scarlet or makes sure the stars shine?

The answer is the Twilight Princess.

She holds two lanterns, each with different fantasies.
The first drips with golden light and
    holds the daydreams,
the things you wish you were doing and
    may well be soon.

The second glows with lapis lazuli shimmers
    and holds good and bad dreams alike,
      visions that make you scream and too afraid
      to sleep as well as perfection,
      dreams so wonderful you refuse to share them.

She collects these dreams of two worlds.

She dances through the night, long
  black hair sailing, gray robes spinning.

When the dawn wakes, she pads home on her bare feet
   to sleep and watch the dreams she's found.

She waits until she's called once more
   to paint the sky with crimson,
   lay down the dawn to sleep,
   remind the night to hang the stars
   to collect and dance with Dreams.

The Twilight Princess…
   Making sure two worlds don't tear apart and die.

LINAEA DIMARINO
Written at age 13

Linaea DiMarino, *The Twilight Princess*

Fire Fairy

Smoke whispered from my wand.
It twirled and whirled —
the wind chimed like a bell,
the leaves rustled —
a soft wind was coming.
A few leaves fell.
A small crunch;
a chipmunk stepped out
from behind a tree.
My mystical world.

HAZEL SECKER
Written at age 8

Hazel Secker, *Fire Fairy*

CHAPTER SEVEN

Who Am I?
Who Are We?

Erin LeBlanc, *Please Don't Hand Me My Soul*,
written at age 14; book page

Please, Don't Hand Me My Soul

Once, a teacher
handed me a template.
Someone else's words.
That an educator
had taken an ax
to,
and directed me to
fill the empty, still-bleeding spaces.
I filled in the borrowed
words, mine,
mixed with the unfortunate
poet's.
And I held out my ink-stained fingers
to her,
and she ignored
my rage,
said "good job,"
and I felt
like I had complied in treason.
And what was left of
my soul
cried black ink
all day.

"Where are all those days no one took a picture of?"*

They're all still there.
Every day you walked to school
on the cold, lifeless sidewalk,
past the stubby, skinny grass
that choked on artificial fumes.
No one thinks to take a picture
of the long car rides back and forth,
of you just sitting there
like a bird on a telephone wire
with thoughts that slip through your head
like heartbeats.
No one took a picture
of the silent, first snowfall last winter,
but you still remember it clearly,
and the heavy, white cushion it hung on the world.
No one took a picture of the rain last Saturday,
and how it fell in thick sheets
off the sides of the buildings,
but I still remember the excitement
that seized up my chest,
and the fact that you were right there beside me.
I figure life isn't supposed to be spent
snapping camera lenses all the time;
the real photos are the ones you take with your heart.

CLAIRE HOLMES
Written at age 13

* From *Words Under the Words* by Naomi Shihab Nye

The Words Out of My Mouth, the Color from my Eyes

I realized I was a cut flower

when his anger-filled eyes came to rest upon me

and I wilted a little.

I was enveloped by his fury,

entirely submerged in shadow,

languishing in the thick silence.

So I tried to speak,

but with a single look,

he had taken my words

and disposed of them neatly,

in color-coordinated piles

at the bottom of the garbage bin.

I warbled out a few incoherent syllables,

which faded into nothing.

So I closed my mouth,

with a soft, resonating thud,

and the world around me lost its vibrancy,

becoming a blurry black and white.

FRIDA ROSNER
Written at age 15

Lily, take me back

to when I was oblivious

to all the problems in the world.

I'm afraid my eyes

have become aware of

every little wrinkle

in the smooth fabric of our planet.

Lily, take me back

to when all I wished to do

was run fast as I could,

my hair flowing out behind me

guided by invisible fingers

of the wind.

Soak me in your petals.

Spread your warmth

throughout my body.

Take me back

to when happiness

was always a close friend.

SHOSHANNA ROSENZWEIG-DAVIDOVITS
Written at age 10

I Come From

I come from love,

love from nature,

love from flowers.

I come from peace,

a relaxed feeling

in my heart.

I come from respect,

respecting others,

respecting myself.

I come from flying

in the blue, sunshiny sky,

imagining I am

a sweet, beautiful hummingbird.

I watch over

everyone with love —

the trees, the sky,

the sun, the flowers,

and all people.

My spirit follows all mankind

like a shadow follows me

as I walk on a sandy path.

KIERSTEN BAYER
Written at age 9

There is a boy

who loves poetry.

The boy only receives good poems

if he listens to his heart.

The boy feels *mindful* and peaceful

as an oak tree standing still

in the middle of a long, grassy meadow.

When the boy opens

the door to *The Poetry Studio,*

he knows many poems

will spread throughout his whole body,

every Wednesday

and every fall.

The boy feels joyful.

Loew Lumbra-Armstrong
Written at age 8

162

I have seen the bleak routine patterns
of human nature.
Time around us was like
a carefully picked judgment.
As adults forgot they were adults,
kids stopped hoping.
They just waited and watched,
their tongues hanging out
like dogs looking for love.

And we watched,
hoping we were more innocent
than we felt.

Ezra Marder
Written at age 14

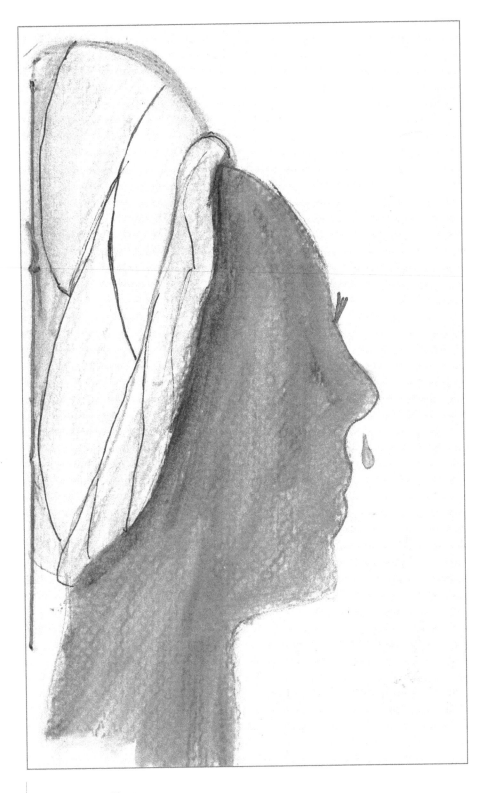

Tae Weiss, *Chains*

Chains

As I look down at my hands,
they are rough and sore
from working in the fields.
From working in misery.
I was born in freedom.
I was raised in freedom.
And all I knew was freedom.
Until the chains came.
The chains wrapped around my ankles.
The chains wrapped around my
happiness.
The chains wrapped around my wrists.
The chains wrapped around my tears.
I tried to pull myself away,
but the chains would not permit it.

I was led off to live in a hut.
I was led off to sleep on the ground.

As I look down at my hands,
I think of my parents, who ran.
They ran with all the others
and yet they were two of the few
who got away.
Who got away from laboring without pay.

They ran with all the others
and yet, they were two of the few
who got away from misery.

As I look down at my hands,
I know what I must do.
I must run out of chains
and into hope.

Tae Weiss
Written at age 12

165

My Broken World

Everything around me is broken.
Earthquakes that leave houses
crumbled like breadcrumbs,
people's spirits cracked
like shattered glass.
I do not understand
why the universe is dawdling
and not fixing
our broken world.

AVA ROSENZWEIG-DAVIDOVITS
Written at age 10

Ella Bathory-Peeler, *Defiled by Society*, title page

Sadness

Sadness
overwhelming me
Someone
has caged my heart
The sky
has disappeared
behind clouds
of stone
The sun
rays of happiness and
laughter
stolen
and imprisoned

In place
of my heart
sadness has brought
a frozen
and wilted flower

She was once beautiful
and happy
her name was Poppy
she wore a dress
of scarlet
her heart now encaged
as mine is
the metal bars
pushing
from every side
and still
we wait
to be released
from sadness

MARIAN WOJCIK
Written at age 10

You see me on the
outside
predictable
You think you know me
the way I play with
my hair when I get nervous
and my constant smile
But that's only half of me
you don't see the hidden
laugh at something you didn't like
raging anger under
my skin that you never see
and the invisible tears
coursing down my cheeks
and the love I'm too
scared to show
You see me on the
outside

ANNELISE FEDORUK
Written at age 10

This morning,
I heard Sweden calling my name.
In my mind,
I can hear the ocean waves
crashing against the shore,
the ocean waves
a sparkling, turquoise blue.
In my mind,
I see the cabin
up the path from the ocean,
where Jorgen, my brother,
sits on a bed,
reading quietly,
as quiet
as a girl writing a poem.
This morning,
I heard Sweden calling my name,
Juan and Eva's voices
making me feel at home.

Tea Sweeney, *Untitled*: "This Morning…," written at age 9; book page

My Grandparents' House

I walk in the door.

I feel the heat from the crimson-red

flames of the fire.

I smell the vegetable broth

bubbling on the stove,

a scent like springtime.

From the kitchen

I hear my grandparents' Swedish voices

as calm

as a leaf fluttering from a tree.

At their home

I feel comfortable,

peaceful,

safe

as jewelry locked in a box.

Jorgen Sweeney
Written at age 9

"Why did you lie to me?" people would say.
I hate that word — *lie*.
It makes you feel fake,
like you're putting on a costume
for the world to see.
I know they felt betrayed,
but how could I fix that?
People look at you differently.
They want to know what you would have been,
if not for your lousy choice of what to be.
I don't like the word "choice"
when, in fact, you had no decision.

EZRA MARDER
Written at age 13

Why Do You Love Me?

Why do you love me?
Is it the way I listen
to all your worries?
Or is it when I sing
to you before bed?
Is that why you love me?

Is it the way I honor your feelings
as much as I honor my own?
Or is it the way I hold you
when you are sad?
Is that why you love me?

Or is it when I'm with you,
I can always be myself?
Is that why you love me?

Meroushka Rosner
Written at age 9

Tae Weiss,
All of Us,
title page

Determined

They say I'm not good enough,
that I'm too different.

They say I get lost in my own

thoughts, that I won't come back.

They say my mind works differently,

that I choose the wrong path.

They say I don't have the power,

yet they have too much.

They say I'm too determined,

that my compass is jumbled up.

But that's just who I am.

Maise Sperling
Written at age 12

Future is a girl of knowledge,

A girl of knowing what will come.

Too afraid to shout it out,

too afraid to tell the truth.

Only waits and watches the world go by.

Looking deep into the souls that litter the world.

Knowing, knowing what will come.

Knowing the truth, knowing the lies.

Not understanding, but understanding completely.

A tear drops, making a stream

that will become a river and an ocean.

But still, nobody knows.

Nobody wants to know.

Nobody cares.

But she knows. She cares.

LILY CHARKEY-BUREN
Written at age 10

Love

Love takes us on a rollercoaster
ups and downs
It goes through objects, pets
and people looking for the one.
It finds something but
it is not the right one.
The mistake breaks my heart
but that is just a lesson.

Love starts to learn.
It makes less mistakes
and my heart starts to heal.
Finally love finds the person
it's been looking for.

My heart gathers
everything love has
collected for me
and finally rests.

Annelise Fedoruk
Written at age 10

Myself

My skin is as smooth
as the inside of a shell.
My eyes are the color
of peppercorns
and as bright as the stars.

Inside, I have silence,
a quiet
like a fallen petal.

When I'm quiet
I sit in a rocking chair
dreaming about summer
on a windy, winter day.

My inside is warm
with love and kindness.

Ann says I listen as carefully
as a deer listening
for a rustle of leaves.

Louisa, a special poet.

LOUISA EICHELBERGER
Written at age 5

Louisa Eichelberger, *Myself*

The Truth about Love

Love,
Love has no end.
It has no pattern.
Love sounds so beautiful
but it is silent.
Love has no shape.
It has a strong voice
though it doesn't speak.

The trees and the flowers celebrate love.
The wind floats through tree leaves
and flowers blossom
weaving a song to love
     that everyone feels.

Love will never end.

MADISON DIMARINO
Written at age 9

I am the guardian

of tree toads,

as small

as a raindrop.

They're so small

you might not notice them.

But I hope my grandchildren

and their grandchildren

will see this gift of nature,

tree toads hopping

and leaping through

the summer grass.

WILLOW WEISS
Written at age 7

My Aunt, Janet

Janet, your spirit seems to say:
Come close to my heart.
Joy streams into my soul.

Janet, even though your body is old,
Your spirit is young and joyful
as a girl dancing with her friends
in a field of laughter.

Janet, when I have an idea
your ears grow bigger and open
like a flower blooming.

Janet, your spirit will always remain in mine.

ROSALIE SMITH
Written at age 8

Rosalie Smith, *My Aunt, Janet*

That Strange Feeling

That strange feeling
that trickles through you
like a stream in your head
and sings a song
that tickles your mind.
That strange feeling
fills you up with thoughts
and questions
that have no answers
and it's hard not to laugh.
That strange feeling
feels like a feather
brushing against your cheek
surprising, but cool.
That strange feeling
sticks in my brain
like honey.

LUNA WEISS
Written at age 10

A few days have passed,
and you have grown up.
No more make-believe
on pirate ships,
or timeless hours at the park.
You skate through childhood,
leaving behind the little boy
you once knew.

Ezra Marder, *Untitled*: "A few days have passed…," written at age 14; book page

Maia Castro-Santos, *Look Closer*

Back to the Shore of Tranquility

Though your sun may only rise
if the gate to your heart is open,

Though your moon may only set
when you find beauty in your sorrow,

Though the ocean may pull you into
a pool of despair,
may you ride the waves
back to the shore of tranquility.

Tae Weiss
Written at age 13

Reflections

Frida Rosner, *The Sunflower Summer*, title page

STUDENTS AND ALUMNI SPEAK

Ella Bathory-Peeler, age 18

I started attending the summer workshops at *The Poetry Studio* when I was 7 years old without a clue as to the role poetry would play in my coming years. I am now 18 years old and use poetry to process my most intense and seemingly unexplainable emotions. The pressure of adolescence and the complexities of mental/emotional growth are greatly underestimated. Children and teenagers are expected to be constantly producing: taking tests and exams, turning in papers, projects, and reflections, yet there is no time factored in for genuine reflection. Poetry has become my medium by which I reflect and dive into myself when the outside world fails to give me the time and space I need to do so. I would be a less centered person without poetry. Without *The Poetry Studio*, I wouldn't have the tranquil, open, and respectful relationship with poetry that I do now. Ann, Tony, Trey, and the many other adults I worked with at *The Poetry Studio* opened their hearts to me in a way that showed respect and honest curiosity to the anxious and scared 7-year-old who hesitantly followed her Mama into the studio doors. Because of their transparency and open-hearts, that worried little girl grew into the confident young woman I am proud to be today. *The Poetry Studio* is my oasis and my place of breath. It is my home I never want to leave and will always return to. It is my place of comfort, introspection, strength, vulnerability, and growth.

Aashna Kinkhabwala, age 22

The Poetry Studio is such a magical place. It brings together so many people in a place of beauty and joy. I remember feeling like being there rejuvenated my soul before I had to go back to school. I was able to see friends I didn't see any other time of the year and just be in the gardens soaking up the sun. It was so easy to write out in those gardens because there was no judgment or stress, only love and nature. The energy surrounding *The Poetry Studio* was always calming, even at the end of the week when we were wrapping up everything. I wish I had spent more time there as a young adult while in high school and college, but somehow there was no time. Time seems to move faster as one gets older and there never seems to be enough of it. I think one of the best parts of *The Poetry Studio* is that time feels like it moves slower, it is easier to just be in the moment and breathe without feeling the pressures of the outside world. I'm grateful to be a part of this amazing studio and that I am able to always carry a small piece of it wherever I go.

Claire Holmes, age 17

My time [at *The Poetry Studio*] has been crucial to my development as a human being. I'm so glad I started at the studio at such a young age and then continued to take classes as I grew up, because what was taught at the studio also applied to the greater world. Not only were we learning how to become poets; we were also learning how to become people. We expressed so much daily gratitude for nature, each other, and ourselves, most of which I don't have time for or make time for in my daily life at school or in general society. I feel at peace in the studio. I was never worried about what others would think of me. I felt safe and accepted, and I was always amazed by how hard everyone worked to create a space full of creativity, appreciation, and love. It feels remarkable to have been able to spend so much time in such a beautifully sacred place.

Rhys McGovern, age 31

The Poetry Studio was a part of my life for many years, and those weeks are still strong in my memory 15 years later. I have only grown in appreciation of all the skills Ann, Tony, and Lara imparted to me — not just the writing and bookbinding, but the practice and effort of introspection and quiet reflection. I learned so much about myself, who I was with others, and who I could be in the world, under the gentle guidance and inspiration of the space Ann and Tony created with each other and throughout their magical gardens.

Em (Hexe) Batchelder, age 31

Ann and Tony gave me permission to be a poet and artist. It has been one of my greatest gifts in life. They took my work seriously, always: through over a decade of their mentorship I learned how to prioritize my commitment to being a maker and writer of things. They have given hundreds of children of all ages the opportunity to believe in themselves. All children deserve to know that they each possess a unique ability to make beauty in a world that desperately needs more of it. I hold the deepest gratitude for Tony and Ann for their lifelong commitment to this work, and for creating a community of young poet-artists that allowed us to feast on the bounty that comes when cultivating mutual respect, joy, and wonderment. All at the perfect speed of beauty at *The Poetry Studio.*

Frida Rosner, age 20

[In conversation with Ann] I'm so glad I spent the time that I did in your poetry classes and [had] the chance to get to know you over the years. I feel really respected by you and listened to. Not to mention, you've given me a really valuable skill to be able to see myself and see beauty in the world and think and write descriptively and honestly. Referring to the word nuance... I think you're on the right track talking about how your teaching is nuanced because that's really key to why it is such a fulfilling experience to be in a Gengarelly poetry program for so many young poets. The lack of too many grammatical or structural rules makes poetic freedom possible.

The nuance also applies to the fact that your teaching style is shaped around the individual, pushing them in directions they're interested in going. Also I think the warm air of the studio (figuratively) should get a brief acknowledgment. I think it's largely due to how you have us conduct ourselves there, being kind to everyone and mingling across age groups and having a focus on having fun. *The Poetry Studio* has a very specific peaceful but energized environment. It's like a safe haven for people to unwind. It's amazing how everyone can be individual with writing what they want to write about, but there's still a really strong sense of unity and community.

Tae Weiss, age 15

I will never forget the gardens, blooming with flowers, the bees and butterflies, and the toads in the cool of the grasses. Every morning me and my sisters were welcomed by the smiles of Ann, Tony, and Trey. Rain or shine, days were filled with friendship, art, and observations expressed through verse. *The Poetry Studio* allowed me to find poetic composition in nature. Some of the best memories of my childhood were spent there.

Luna Weiss, age 14

I've gone to Ann and Tony's poetry camp since I was 7 years old. Now I am 14. I remember sitting under the trees writing about the flowers and trees and my connection to them. My first poem was about my mother, the hydrangea. She raised me to be me. I talked about her large white flowers protecting me, making a shield of warmth for me. We would share our poems at the end of the time we had to write them. I was always nervous at first but then over the years it turned to excitement about hearing the other people's poetry; hearing about their connection to the willow tree down the hill or the frog pond where they sat on the bench watching the frogs swim or maybe even the thoughts they had about a book they had recently read. Working with Tony was such a pleasure. His warmth and great ideas gave us kids more confidence to go above and beyond for our book work. Each book always turned out [to be] very unique and special in its own way. The conversations we would have working together on our books were always held together and we would all be a part of [them]. Ann has a magical presence about her. She made me feel welcome and safe whenever I was at *The Poetry Studio.* She inspired us to persist and keep…writing out our feelings and what we held inside of us even if we were too scared to let it out on our own. Over these years *The Poetry Studio* has given me the amazing power to create a piece of writing that makes me feel proud of the work that I put into it and, most importantly, the meaning of it and what it teaches me.

Harry Poster, age 32

When I was a smaller little boy I was very worried that everyone could see what I was feeling, or hear my opinions before I spoke them. I knew that if that were true, no one would understand or like me. Because of this I worked hard to not betray myself. Luckily there was a protected space very close to where I lived—where I was invited to be specific and put all of my fear of being misunderstood into words. I was asked if a word I didn't know sounded like what I meant, and if not, implored to find the word that did. I was told that I could be ambiguous now, but later I had a chance to use poetry scissors to remove the unnecessary language. I was taught a craft of writing on terms that didn't intimidate or condescend. Along the way I discovered the unique voices of poets from around the world—one of them being my own. I was given agency to speak; at seven, at twelve, at sixteen, and I was given a studio where I learned how to create. The poetry studio was my first professional residency, and I started working there in first grade. I am a lucky alum of a studio for growing poets and artists of any age. I cannot imagine where I'd be without that home. Thank you, Ann. Thank you, Tony.

AFTERWORD

*A*nother World was scheduled to be launched October 2019. Like so many other events and publications, the book's debut needed to be reconfigured due to Covid-19. Poets who were in fifth grade are now in middle school. Poets then in high school are now in college. Considering their poetry and art once again, we find their voices continue to be true and compelling.

As educators, parents, artists, can we create intentional spaces where our youth — through poetry, story, art — express their diverse responses to this challenging time in history? To have opportunities that offer a shape to our students' thoughts and emotions is critical not only for their well-being but also for generations to come.

Vital questions have pushed through the cracks of the pandemic: How to evoke compassion and create community stand out among the many significant ones.

The Poetry Studio: Gardens in Late Afternoon, August

Can we imagine the language of poetry and art as ways to navigate these pressing social issues? If we are to build a healthier place in the world for everyone, might the creation of a poem or a drawing offer a symbolic way to get close enough to wrap our arms around people who have experienced injustice or unbearable loss?* At the same time, can we pause in our lives to celebrate the persistent beauty of nature; to draw strength from benevolent words and acts, from kinship with the world?

Entering another season, we share a concern about the emotional health of young people who have spent countless hours alone before the screen rather than laughing with a friend or listening in class to a teacher read a story. Many have experienced *pandemic loneliness*. Powerful connections from a poem and drawing shared can span the empty spaces in our lives and provide ways to interact with the larger community. To raise the human spirit through poetry and art should not be considered as a question; rather, it is imperative that the voices from this book tap us on the shoulder, reminding us that our children's creative expression can be a compass for how we should travel from today into all the tomorrows.

Returning once more to the question of community, we recall conversations shared with the young poets and artists on the last day of our summer intensives. Close your eyes and imagine young people ranging in age from 5-16 sitting in a circle on the grass among the gardens. It is during this contemplative time that we often posit questions such as "What will stay with you after this week at *The Poetry Studio*?" "What will you bring home with you?" The students talk about their rich and layered poetry, their beautiful hand-crafted books, but what is stressed even more is their experience of community — their feeling "at home;" enjoying the freedom to be their authentic selves and be totally accepted, feeling safe. It is these responses, these emotions that deeply punctuate this ritual sharing. Their words linger, and we feel a deep gratitude, for it is our youth who invite us to see with innocent eyes; ultimately, they are our mentors, guiding us back into what we know as true. May we all rediscover *Another World* where "Poppy, scarlet chalice / can have nothing to do with our blood-stained newsprint… and the daylilies / tender golden trumpets, / do not voice / the harsh call of war."

---

*In his book *Just Mercy*, Brian Stevenson, founder and executive director of the Equal Justice Initiative, writes about "staying proximate" recalling his grandmother's advice: "You can't understand the most important things from a distance…. you have to get close." This quote from the 2020 virtual Literary Festival in Brattleboro, Vermont, during a session titled "Poetry and Social Justice" carries Stevenson's admonition further: "In a situation where we can't act, we write poetry…. poetry allows us to come close." And the words of Joy Harjo in her description of the poet-warrior come to mind as well: "The poet's road is a journey for truth, for justice…. Compassion is the first quality of a warrior" (from *How We Became Human*, "Introduction").

GRATITUDE

We would like to take this opportunity to acknowledge the work of so many who have made the publication of *Another World* possible; our friends near and far whose support, in too many ways to name, helped our dream become the book you now hold in your hands. From hanging exhibits of the students' work to accompanying us as these shows slowly evolved into a manuscript, to offering advice regarding the ins and outs of the publishing world — for all this and more we are deeply grateful. You listened and when discouragement might have closed the doors to *Another World* becoming a reality, you showed us the critical nature of persevering.

Among those to whom we are indebted, special thanks to the parents and families whose belief in *The Poetry Studio* inspired them to drive several hours to make participation in our Poetry/Bookmaking program possible for their daughters and sons. Thank you to all the families for your enthusiasm and support and, of course, to our students whose work is the essence of this book — our "Dedication" pays them the tribute they justly deserve.

The gift of Trey Wentworth entering *The Poetry Studio* over 10 years ago cannot be measured. Assistant teacher during many of the after-school programs and in our summer Poetry/Bookmaking workshops, Trey understands the tone of our work, seamlessly traveling between mentoring the young poets and helping with the bookmaking and art as well. The collaboration with Trey allows us to spend more quality time with each student; something not only we appreciate, but also benefits the students.

During the poetry classes, Trey embodies the practice of sharing a dialogue with reverence; always *present* for what a particular student might need. Trey's sensibilities regarding the creative process; a deep respect for each student's unique voice; a love of language and an understanding of the delicate conversation that occurs between poet and mentor; all this and more has made Trey an indispensable part of *The Poetry Studio*.

Trey's willingness to help with the bookmaking classes is much appreciated too. Trey's grasp of the technical challenges and a quick eye for the student who is struggling are invaluable assets through the often-complicated process of creating a book.

Several years ago we first introduced the students' art and poetry to Mara Williams, Chief Curator of the Brattleboro Museum & Art Center. Witnessing the work from *The Poetry Studio* — the poems, the illustrative art, and beautiful handcrafted books that accompanied the students' poetry during a 2015 exhibition at the River Garden gallery — Mara shared with us the inspiration to create an exhibit at the BMAC that would showcase the original and extraordinary work of these young people. This was the birth of the exhibit "Windows to Creative Expression" which opened September 30, 2016.

It was our good fortune that Chard deNiord was selected as the poet laureate of Vermont that same year. Once again it was Mara's vision to involve Chard in this exhibit. It is difficult to recall all the details, but we do remember Chard's visit to *The Poetry Studio* and his excitement upon discovering the students' remarkable voices. This confluence of events led to an invitation for Chard to write the introductory text and brochure essay for our BMAC exhibit.

Chard's faithful support over the years and his nudging us to create a book inspired by the exhibit have helped to make *Another World* a reality. There are no sufficient words to convey the depth of our gratitude to Chard, who in spite of his busy life as the poet laureate met with us regularly to read the students' poetry and offer his insights regarding which poems would be good candidates for *Another World*.

Every poem in this book has been selected with the help of various authors in the Brattleboro area who, beginning with the exhibit at the BMAC (which required that the poems and art be juried) spent long and focused time considering the students' writing. Thanks to Karen Hesse and Arlene Distler who graciously offered their opinions regarding the quality of each poem; this required both a generosity of time and a generosity of spirit. Thanks as well to Trey for his thoughtful insights regarding the students' poems.

We are also grateful to BMAC Director Danny Lichtenfeld and Exhibitions Manager Sarah Freeman who supported "Windows to Creative Expression," giving *The Poetry Studio* its first major public recognition.

We are especially thankful to Karen Hesse who sat with us at Hazel's, a coffee shop in Brattleboro, encouraging us as we pursued the challenging twists and turns of the journey through the world of publishing. We also owe a more specific thank-you to Karen who read Ann's essay "Birthing Poetry," commenting on what she, as a reader, would want to know about the creative process that led to the poems in the book. Gratitude to another reader, Nancy Olson, whose comments prompted the addition of a personal story she had heard during our adult poetry classes. Special appreciation to Nancy Rallis who read and reread the essay, specifically pointing out the parts that resonated with her.

Thanks once more to Nancy Olson, Trey Wentworth, and Arlene Distler who, along with Julie Dolan, enthusiastically took on the role of "Guardian Poets," reading students' poems at the BMAC celebration connected to the *Brattleboro Literary Festival*, October 2016.

Gratitude to Bruce Smith, who over the years has shared his enthusiasm for the young people's poetry. In Ann's words, "Often I have sent Bruce copies of a young person's poem that especially moved me. Always Bruce would respond with his inimitable way of demonstrating his respect for the students' work." Special thanks for his faithful reminders of the importance of creating a safe space for students to have a voice.

A special mention for Jamie Franklin, Director of Exhibitions and Collections, and Deana Mallory, Director of Public Programs, at the Bennington Museum for their inspiration and support as this project unfolded. Their expertise with and promotion of the art of young people has expanded our awareness of the connections between word and image.

To Naomi Shihab Nye and James Crews, who not only wrote inspiring blurbs for the book's cover, but also offered compassion during moments of discouragement; a deep bow to their wholehearted support of the vision that was our guiding light for sharing the young people's poetry and art in *Another World*.

To the Antioch Graduate Interns and numerous assistant teachers — friends and mentors — especially Saint Rosner, Em (Hexe) Batchelder, and Aryars Hemphill as well as Robin MacArthur, Frida Rosner, Julie Erickson, Patricia Austen, Brin Tucker, and Ellie Oliver who graciously offered their gifts and talents to the *Studio*. Their energy and enthusiasm have helped lift our efforts over the past several years.

Profound thanks to Miriam Dror and Etta Shirley (principal of Little Singer School on the Navajo Nation) for inspiration and for modeling the power of intergenerational community.

Special gratitude to Barbara Charkey, Lorni Cochran, Richard Dror, Paul Evelti, Liza Ketchum, Miriam Maracek, Jennifer and Joe Mazur, Petey Mitchell, Nancy Rallis, as well as Robbie Merfeld and Anya Shemetyeva for being fellow travelers on this journey; who listened attentively to our concerns and offered thoughtful and wise counsel when asked.

We also greatly appreciate the participants from the adult poetry classes who followed us every step of the way with encouragement and support. We would also like to acknowledge the invaluable efforts of Lucinda Dee, Ray Warren, and Nancy Olson who helped with the installation of the first showing of the students' work at the River Garden in Brattleboro, which ultimately led to the BMAC exhibit and the creation of *Another World*.

To our Poetry Studio alumni, too numerous to list here, whose words and images are still with us on these pages and in our hearts.

Heartfelt gratitude to our daughter, Lara, for the many hours she spent reading the raw beginnings of what has turned into a book. A former co-teacher for the summer workshops at *The Poetry Studio*, her encouragement and wise counsel has certainly helped to shape a more coherent and inspirational book. A special thank-you to our son-in-law Al Pratt and our grandchildren Norah and Elias for listening to and commenting on the students' poems as we created piles on the table or floor for this chapter or that.

To Madeline Bergstrom and Liz Bergstrom of Bobolink Communications who not only superbly edited our prose, but also expressed the joy they felt as they read the students' poetry and looked at their art.

To Claire Flint Last who designed the beautiful cover and honored the students' poetry and art with her striking interior design of this book; thanks also to those at Luminare Press who published *Another World*, especially Patricia Marshall who recognized the book's unique qualities and Kim Harper Kennedy, who guided the process to completion.

To John DiGeorge and Frida Rosner for their artful contribution of *The Poetry Studio* logo.

Finally, an eternal debt of gratitude to Hannah Christensen whose poem *Another World* has been our faithful companion and inspiration.

ABOUT THE AUTHORS

Ann Gengarelly

Since 1980, Ann Gengarelly has been a poet-in-the schools throughout South-eastern Vermont and neighboring Massachusetts and New Hampshire.

She is Director of *The Poetry Studio* at her home in Marlboro, Vermont, where during the past twenty-five years she has offered after-school programs in poetry and art for students from kindergarten to eighth grade. *The Studio* also runs summer workshops that feature poetry, art, and bookmaking with a focus on the natural world.

Since 2002, Ann has taught studio creative writing classes for adults as well. Gathering together, participants ranging in age from their 20s to 70s create a rich and extraordinary community.

She has had the privilege to teach poetry workshops (2000-2010) on the Navajo Nation at Little Singer Community School in Bird Springs, Arizona. In many ways the indigenous practice of community—the inclusion of young people with elders—has informed the composition of her *Studio* classes.

Ann's connection to indigenous ways began when, under the auspices of the American Friends Service Committee, she spent a summer working on the Cherokee Nation in the smoky mountains of North Carolina.

For seven years Ann was a Faculty Associate at Hampshire College where she offered courses such as "Creativity and the Young Child" and "Integrative Seminar: The Creative Process." She has been a consultant for the Integrated Day Program at the University of Massachusetts. Using poetry as a model, Ann has designed and presented professional development workshops for teachers at Lesley University, Bank Street College, and the Antioch NE Graduate School of Education.

Ann holds an MA degree from Goddard College in creativity and education with an emphasis on poetry-in-the schools. She received an honorary degree for Teaching Excellence from Marlboro College in 1988.

She has published in numerous poetry and professional journals ranging from *The Apple Tree Review* and *Birmingham Arts Journal* to *The Elementary School Journal* (University of Chicago Press) and *Literary Cavalcade* (*Scholastic Magazine*).

In a recent conversation with one of her grandchildren, she found herself mentioning that in the past she thought she was going to be a social worker. The child responded: "But you *are* a social worker; you get people to express their emotions;" these words capturing the essence of Ann's teaching, whether she is in a high school dormitory on the Navajo Nation or teaching among her gardens in Marlboro, Vermont.

Tony Gengarelly

Tony Gengarelly is Professor Emeritus of Fine Arts at Massachusetts College of Liberal Arts. His academic background and interests are varied. Along with survey courses in American Civilization and Western Art History, his teaching career has included literature, political science, modern and decorative art, and museum studies. He has also taught on the Navajo Nation and introduced Diné weaving and sandpainting, along with the Santero art of the American Southwest, to his college students. For the past several years his work has focused on the creative process and its social and cultural crosscurrents.

Tony is the founder and current Director of the Jessica Park Project at MCLA. Based on the career of Jessica Park, a visionary artist on the autism spectrum, the Project partners with college students and professors, museum curators, and educators to explore the subject of Outsider Art, which features artists who, as a result of circumstance and place, stand apart from the aesthetic and cultural mainstream.

Since 1999 Tony has taught art and bookmaking for *The Poetry Studio*'s summer workshops. He has been especially impressed by the "outsider" features of the young people's art: its unfettered focus and originality; its direct communication of complex ideas and strong emotions through color and line; its use of visual language with creative and powerful expression.

Tony has curated individually or produced with his students over 40 exhibitions. Some of these have been featured at the Sterling and Francine Clark Art Institute, Williams College Museum of Art, MCLA Gallery 51, Brattleboro Museum & Art Center, Endicott College, Eastern Michigan University, Wheaton College, and the 94 Porter Street Gallery at MCLA.

Chloe Rosner, *Never underestimate the power of imagination,* book page pop-up

Tony has written and published on a variety of subjects, including Political Justice, Early American Modernism, Native American painting, and Outsider Art. Most noteworthy are articles for the *Mind's Eye* and *Folk Art Messenger;* also contributions on poster art for *The Guide to United States Popular Culture* (Bowling Green State University Press) and Maurice Prendergast's applied graphic art for *A Catalogue Raisonne* (Williams College Museum of Art; Prestel Books). He has edited and written two books on the art of Jessica Park (*Exploring Nirvana*, MCLA 2008; *A World Transformed*, MCLA 2014). Other books include *Art on the Spectrum: A Guide for Mentoring and Marketing Artists with ASD* (KDP Amazon, 2020); *Randy Trabold's Northern Berkshire County* (Arcadia, 2003); *Distinguished Dissenters and Opposition to the 1919-1920 Red Scare* (Edwin Mellen, 1996).

Tony holds a Ph.D. in American and New England Studies from Boston University and a MA from Williams College in the history of art.

Hazel Secker writing on the porch at The Poetry Studio

Anything that matters is here.
Anything that will continue to matter
in the next several thousand years
will continue to be here.   Approaching
in the distance is the child you were
some years ago.   See her laughing as
she chases a white butterfly.

Joy Harjo